T0344951

Project Finance

Project Finance

Applications and Insights to Emerging Markets Infrastructure

Paul D. Clifford

WILEY

Published by John Wiley & Sons, Inc., Hoboken, New Jersey.
Published simultaneously in Canada.

For general information on our other products and services or for technical support, please contact our Customer Care Department within the United States at (800) 762-2974, outside the United States at (317) 572-3993, or fax (317) 572-4002.

Wiley publishes in a variety of print and electronic formats and by print-on-demand. Some material included with standard print versions of this book may not be included in e-books or in print-on-demand. If this book refers to media such as a CD or DVD that is not included in the version you purchased, you may download this material at http://booksupport.wiley.com. For more information about Wiley products, visit www.wiley.com.

Library of Congress Cataloging-in-Publication Data

Names: Clifford, Paul D., author. | John Wiley & Sons, Inc., publisher.
Title: Project finance : applications and insights to emerging markets infrastructure / Paul D. Clifford.
Description: Hoboken, New Jersey : Wiley, [2021] | Includes bibliographical references and index.
Identifiers: LCCN 2020033757 (print) | LCCN 2020033758 (ebook) | ISBN 9781119642466 (hardback) | ISBN 9781119642541 (adobe pdf) | ISBN 9781119642572 (epub)
Subjects: LCSH: Infrastructure (Economics)—Finance. | Project finance—Developing countries. | Economic development projects—Finance.
Classification: LCC HC79.C3 C575 2021 (print) | LCC HC79.C3 (ebook) | DDC 332.609172/4—dc23
LC record available at https://lccn.loc.gov/2020033757
LC ebook record available at https://lccn.loc.gov/2020033758

Cover image: © alexey_boldi/Getty Images
Cover design: Wiley

Printed in the United States of America.

SKY10021797_102120

Marie

Contents

Preface

Infrastructure investment needs are forecast to be approximately $3.5–3.8 trillion per year through 2040, with over 60 percent of this demand in emerging markets. Indeed, infrastructure investment is a proven and critical enabler of socioeconomic development. Project finance provides the key financing paradigm for unlocking the investment capital required to deliver this growing demand for infrastructure investment, particularly in developing countries.

When I first came to this field through the private sector in the early 1990s, little was written on the subject, and I often found myself working and learning by doing. The genesis for this book derived from the insights I gained "in the trenches" along with my years teaching a bespoke infrastructure and project finance course to Columbia University MBA students. *Project Finance: Applications and Insights to Emerging Market Infrastructure* fills this knowledge gap between years of private sector experience and academic scholarship. It covers the fundamentals and principles of applying project finance structuring to emerging markets, supplemented and supported by seminal emerging market case studies, along with my own experience over 20 years advising, structuring, and executing project finance transactions in key developing countries across Asia, Africa, and South America. The book also addresses important current topics such as China's Belt and Road Initiative as well as new trends and developments in the project and infrastructure sector such as impact investing, UN Social Development Goals, the emergence of new global multilateral development banks, renewable energy, and green bonds. My hope is to offer an accessible, comprehensive introduction of the subject from a practitioner's perspective across students, academics, and public and private sector finance professionals involved with, or interested in, project finance and infrastructure investment in emerging markets.

I have structured the book into three major sections: an introduction to the foundational principles and key qualitative and quantitative project finance structuring tools, application of these techniques to projects in emerging markets, and finally a discussion on the current developments in the project finance market.

- *Introduction and general background on project finance along with discussion and insights on asset class performance and sizing the emerging markets infrastructure gap.*

  - Chapter 1 provides a brief history on the origins, uses, and applications of project finance, what defines project finance, along with an overview of the performance of project finance as an asset class and defining the infrastructure gap in developing countries;

  - Chapter 2 covers project finance risks and how to analyze, mitigate, and allocate those key risks to project parties. The Mozal, Mozambique, project case study demonstrates how effective project finance contract risk allocation is used to de-risk projects.

  - Chapter 3 addresses key project finance agreements, loan documentation, and project security along with the key loan structural features and term sheet negotiation strategies for lenders and investors. The Samba, Brazil, project case study highlights how a project finance security package and related structural features operate in practice.

- *Application and implementation of project finance in emerging markets, critical sources of financing, and financial modeling and important debt sizing quantitative techniques.*

  - Chapter 4 reviews the track record and key lessons learned from emerging markets project finance. The Dabhol, India, power project provides valuable insights on the risks and challenges for large-scale infrastructure projects in emerging markets.

  - Chapter 5 offers a comprehensive review of the main sources of project finance for infrastructure investments and the relative pros and cons with each source of financing. The Nam Theun 2, Laos/Thailand, project case study illustrates how superior execution of a complex multi-source project financing can be achieved.

  - Chapter 6 provides a primer on financial modeling from both debt and equity investor perspectives along with debt sizing, application, and interpretation of debt service coverage ratios and loan amortization techniques. The Sabine Pass LNG, USA, project highlights the effective use of bank loans and project bonds in the finance plan.

- *Discussion on environment, social, and governance, UN SDG's and impact investing, tapping debt capital markets and project bonds, the scope and objectives of China's Belt and Road Initiative, and new and emerging project finance structures and market trends.*

- Chapter 7 addresses sustainable project finance and infrastructure investment, the origins and applications of Equator Principles by commercial banks, the current trends and developments concerning impact investing, ESG-linked lending, and green bonds. The Manzanillo, Mexico, project illustrates the important role played by multilateral development banks in addressing and mitigating ESG risks.
- Chapter 8 covers debt capital markets and project bonds, the key institutional investors in project bonds, the merits and drawbacks of project bonds versus bank loans, as well as structuring and execution issues. The Mong Duong, Vietnam, project showcases a successful project bond refinancing in a frontier emerging market.
- Chapter 9 focuses on China's Belt and Road Initiative, the scope and key components of the largest and most ambitious infrastructure investment initiative ever undertaken along with the strategic, commercial, economic, and financial objectives of China. The challenge of financing the Belt and Road Initiative is addressed along with a profile of the new multilateral development banks and other financial institutions established to assist with the required funding.
- Chapter 10 spotlights a number of key project finance structures and market developments including the advent of min-perm structures, multilateral development bank credit enhancement guarantees to mobilize institutional investor capital, and back-levered debt structures.

Acknowledgments

The germ of the idea for this book was nurtured over many years and decades working with, and learning from, wonderful colleagues, friends, mentors, and peers. I will be eternally grateful to the many people who helped shape the contours of this volume, without whom it would not have come to fruition. Nikita Baryshnikov and Michael Whalen generously read, reviewed, and provided invaluable feedback, encouragement, and guidance throughout the development of this book. I would also like to thank Columbia University Business School for the opportunity and privilege to teach my project finance and infrastructure course: it provided the ideal forum to test and forge many of the principles and ideas in the book with a brilliant and engaging cadre of students. Thanks also to Columbia Business School MBA student Rafael Matos for helping with formatting certain charts and tables. I am immensely grateful for the assistance and support provided by McKinsey & Company, Standard & Poor's, The World Bank, the Asian Development Bank, the Global Infrastructure Hub, Refinitiv, and the Climate Bond Initiative for allowing me to draw on their research material for the book. A special thanks to friends and associates, in particular Sergio Sanz and Conor McCoole, for their wise counsel and advice. Thanks also to Susan Cerra, Samantha Enders, Richard Samson, Mike Henton, and all of the editorial team at Wiley Publishing for their unstinting commitment and support during the writing process. Finally, I would like to thank my family and friends, especially my wife and fellow academic and published author Laura, without whose encouragement, support, and belief this book would not have seen the light of day. To the rest of my family and my children Haley and Darcy for your unwavering support and love, which sustained me over the last year writing this book. Thank you one and all.

CHAPTER 1

Principles and Application of Project Finance

ORIGINS AND HISTORY OF PROJECT FINANCE

Project finance is a highly versatile, if often misunderstood and misapplied, financing paradigm. There is no one single definition that succinctly captures project finance. Ostensibly, it is the long-term financing of infrastructure and industrial projects based upon the projected cash flows of the underlying project rather than the balance sheet of the project sponsors. Project finance refers to the financing of long asset life infrastructure, industrial and public assets, and services using non- or limited-recourse financing raised by an enterprise with a single line of business/finite asset life in accordance with contractual agreements.

Project finance is a tried and tested financial discipline that has been around for many centuries. The history and origins of project finance can be traced back to the 13th century when Italian banks financed a silver mine in Devon, England, with the loan repayment source being a lease over physical silver production from the mine. It has been used to finance maritime voyages to the new world in the 17th and 18th centuries with the merchant investors dividing the cargo spoils from returning ships. Project finance's application to infrastructure can be traced to the original construction of the Panama Canal and was key to financing wildcat upstream oil and gas investments in the early 19th century in the US along with the development of the North Sea oil fields in the 1970s and 1980s. The seminal market development that established the modern version of long-term contract-based project financing was the oil crisis in the US in the early 1970s. The fears and concerns over energy dependence forged the passage of the Public Utilities Regulatory Policy Act (PURPA) in the US in 1978. PURPA served to open the US electricity market to non-utility generators (NUGs) in an effort to increase energy supply, which heralded the origins of deregulation of the US electricity sector. PURPA essentially required vertically integrated monopoly utilities to purchase power from NUGs at their "avoided cost," which is the cost a utility would pay to generate power itself. This opened the energy market up to what became known globally as the Independent Power Producer (IPP) market and created the ability to raise project financing on the back of long-term power purchase agreements with creditworthy electricity purchaser utilities.

WHY SPONSORS USE PROJECT FINANCE

Project finance is both a financing and a governance structure. It is based on the notion that project risks are identified upfront, allocated to those best able to bear them, and mitigated such that the residual risks are acceptable to lenders. While project finance risk analysis and mitigation is not unique to this asset class, the process of contractual allocation of risk is unique to project finance. Project finance is sometimes referred to as "contract financing." The scope of the project along with the financing and security arrangements granted to lenders are set out in a comprehensive set of contractual documents entered into by the project company—and identified project risks are effectively allocated to those parties best able to bear them via these project contracts.

While there are many and varied reasons why project sponsors choose to use project financing versus on balance sheet corporate financing, according to Benjamin Esty it is to reduce capital markets imperfections or the net costs associated with the following:[1]

- **Transaction Costs:** Project finance deals generally take anywhere from 6 to 12 months to structure, negotiate, and execute the financing. The incremental legal, financial, and other costs associated with execution of the project financing can represent, on average, anywhere from 3% to 5% of total project costs. As such, transaction costs for project finance deals exceed comparable costs for corporate-financed deals.

- *Asymmetric Information:* Project finance capital providers to a greenfield infrastructure project—which is highly leveraged, thinly capitalized, and typically a single-asset special purpose company with no cash flows—require extra due diligence (independent consultants, insurance/legal advisors, and financial modeling), reporting, and controls (cash flow waterfall, financial and non-financial covenants, step-in rights, pledge of security/contracts, etc.). This reduces asymmetric information between lenders and owners/sponsors. The robust due diligence process that project finance lenders undertake also ensures that negative net present value (NPV) projects will not be undertaken as would be the case in corporate deals where project cash flows are co-mingled, fungible, and subject to cross-subsidizing between positive and negative NPV projects.

- *Incentive/Agency Conflicts:* Project finance helps reduce incentive/agency conflicts due to higher leverage/risk of default and assignment of most of the project cash flows toward servicing debt. This dissuades stakeholders (shareholders, governments, construction companies, operators, etc.) from cash flow diversion actions that would negatively affect the project. The high risk and high leverage typical of project finance deals would normally mean investors and creditors would require higher risk adjusted returns (as measured by the internal rate of return, or IRR) and a higher risk premium on debt, which in turn requires larger project cash flows and heightens the risk of stakeholder interference and adverse actions. The contract structuring and associated risk allocation, which is the essence of project finance, serves to mitigate and reduce risk and therefore reduce required project returns by investors and creditors, which in turn lowers incentive conflict.

- *Financial Distress:* Project finance reduces or eliminates project sponsor risk contamination as the legally independent special purpose vehicle (SPV) project borrower ensures the project debt is "off balance sheet" to the sponsor from an accounting treatment perspective. It is more difficult to achieve full "off credit risk" treatment as credit rating agencies typically take the view that the debt and the underlying project is an intrinsic and strategically core part part of the sponsor company's business operations. The sponsor would be viewed as never exercising its non-recourse rights ("walking away") should the project default. It is one of the main reasons integrated oil and gas majors such as Xon and Chevron typically do not use project financing unless they need to accommodate a financially weaker joint venture partner or are seeking to mitigate country risk. However, it is exactly why a company like US IPP Calpine Corp with 95% debt-to-equity and a sub-investment grade rating was able to successfully raise $5 billion in project finance loans to construct 25 new power generation plants in the early 2000s.

PROJECT FINANCE—ASSET CLASS PERFORMANCE

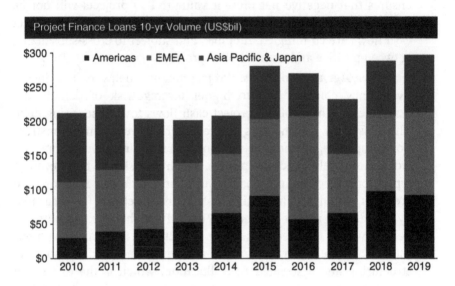

Project Finance Loans 10-yr Volume (US$bil)

Source: Refinitiv 2019 Global Project Finance Review.

The global project finance market is relatively small—the total project finance loan market amounted to $297 billion in 2019—relative to the US leveraged loan market ($1.6 trillion) or the US capital markets ($3 trillion).[2] That said, project finance is a critical lynchpin for catalyzing and crowding in other forms of private sector capital (insurance companies, pension funds, infrastructure funds, sovereign wealth funds, private equity, etc.) along with development financial institutions (DFIs) such as multilateral and bilateral development banks and export credit agencies.

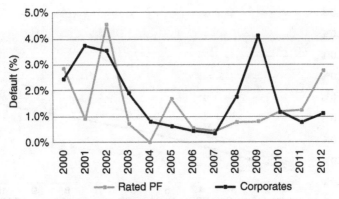

Source: S&P Global Market Intelligence, Annual Global Project Finance Default and Recovery Study, 1980-2014 (S&P Global Market Intelligence, 2016).

Notwithstanding that project finance involves financing a thinly capitalized, high leveraged single asset with no cash flows and material construction risks, it has proven to be a resilient asset class able to withstand adverse, unexpected external events. A Standard & Poor's (S&P) 2016 study analyzed project finance default rates and recovery from 1980 to 2014.[3] The study covered over 8,000 projects across all industries and geographies. The S&P study revealed that the project finance annual default rate peaked in 2002–03 at around 4.8%; however, since then the annual default rate has averaged 1.5% per annum compared to 1.8% annual average default rate for secured corporate lending. The 2002–03 peak in project finance defaults resulted from the following coterminous macroeconomic events:

- The 2001 Argentina sovereign debt default and currency devaluation, which negatively affected natural resource (mainly oil and gas) and power projects;
- The 2002 US energy crisis resulting from the bankruptcy of Enron (at the time the largest corporate bankruptcy in US history), which caused the US and European energy markets to decline, resulting in increased project defaults and the demise of the merchant power sector;
- The 2002 dot-com Internet asset bubble collapse, resulting in telecom corporate defaults (WorldCom, Global Crossing, etc.)

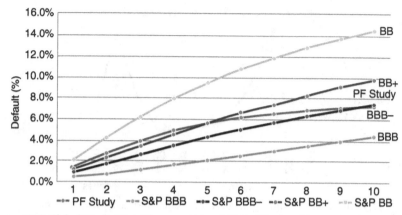

Source: S&P Global Market Intelligence, Annual Global Project Finance Default and Recovery Study, 1980-2014 (S&P Global Market Intelligence, 2016).

The S&P study found that the annual marginal default rate for the project finance deals correlated to a sub-investment grade double B rating in years 1–3 following financial close and trended toward single A investment grade by year 10. The study also confirms that highest project risk is in the first 3–5 years during the construction period and initial operational ramp-up. Default rates fall dramatically after year 5 as an operational track record is achieved and stable cash flows are established such that the 10-year cumulative default rate equates to triple B investment grade rating. Approximately 75% of all project finance loan defaults occur in the first 5 years. Annual marginal default rates decline dramatically after year 3–5, and by year 10 they are close to single A-rated corporate issuers. Not surprisingly the majority of project finance loan defaults occurred in the power sector (36%) due to the historic collapse of the US merchant power sector and effect of the Enron default as well as renewable energy loan defaults in Europe due to reduction/elimination of subsidies and feed-in-tariffs arising from fiscal austerity measures implemented by Spain and Italy and other countries in the aftermath of the 2008 financial crisis. Infrastructure project defaults were 24% due mainly to the spike in toll road loan defaults in European countries (Greece, Portugal, Italy, Spain) following the 2008 financial crisis. Despite thin capitalization, high gearing, and long loan tenors, project finance loans are structured to be very robust and resilient to a wide range of potential risk events and to minimize any post-default economic losses. The S&P study demonstrates that risk allocation, structural features, underwriting disciplines, and incentive allignments have proved effective. The key structural features of project finance loans that serve to reduce default risk include:

Effective Contractual Risk Allocation: Construction risk is typically mitigated via fixed price, date-certain turnkey Engineering, Procurement, and Construction (EPC) contracts with performance guarantees and liquidated damages (LDs) or penalties for delay and performance shortfalls. Revenue risk is typically addressed via predictable, resilient cash flow streams based on long-term offtake contracts with firm take or pay obligations provided by strong, creditworthy offtakers. Demand/volume risk and price risks are typically risk transferred to the offtaker. Project finance lenders do not finance against the full term of the offtake contract and usually require a 2–3 year "contract tail" between the loan maturity date and the offtake contract termination date.

Covenant Structure: Serves to control the project scope and constrains the project company against deviating from its core business activity. Protective forward-looking covenants, reserve accounts, cash traps/cash sweeps, dividends distributions tests, and other structural features mitigate liquidity risk. These measures serve to insulate the project from unexpected cash flow stress scenarios.

Project Due Diligence: Lenders' advisors (independent technical consultant, market consultant, legal advisor, insurance consultant, etc.) produce due diligence reports identifying all risks and recommend risk allocation/mitigation. Effective risk allocation is materially achieved in large part via detailed due diligence and appraisal of project life cycle operational and maintenance costs. Detailed financial models are developed using lenders base case assumptions and stress test sensitivity analysis derived from the various due diligence reports. The third-party due diligence also ensures that negative NPV projects are not undertaken.

Detailed Terms Sheet and Negotiation of Financial Terms: The rigorous and robust term sheet negotiations between lenders and project sponsors ensures that all risks are identified/allocated/mitigated such that residual risk is within acceptable parameters (i.e., bankable). The integration of the due diligence risk identification and the underlying project finance model provides a comprehensive basis for detailed negotiations and agreement on lending terms and conditions between project sponsors and lenders. This serves to ensure that all critical risks are clearly allocated and assigned such that residual risks that remain with the project borrower are acceptable to lenders.

Proactive Monitoring by Agents: The scope of information reporting/monitoring in project finance is much greater compared to corporate lending. During the construction period, for example, project finance borrowers are typically required to furnish monthly construction reports to lenders, and in some cases the loan distributions during construction are subject to "cost to complete" tests by the lenders' independent engineer to ensure there are sufficient debt and equity proceeds available to complete the project. Physical and financial completion tests (typically 90 days) may also be required by lenders and subject to the independent engineer's sign off. Monitoring and reporting requirements during the operational period include quarterly financial reports, notice of any material changes or developments, compliance with negative and positive covenants, as well as financial covenant tests when the cash flow waterfall is run every quarter or semi-annually (minimum Debt Service Coverage Ratio, or DSCR, maintenance of a Debt Service Reserve Account, dividend distrubution tests, etc.).

The S&P study indicates that post-default project finance loans achieve a high loan recovery rate—averaging 79.5%, or almost 80 cents on the dollar—with ultimate loan recovery rates much higher for restructuring/workouts versus distressed loan asset sales. The loan recovery rates for project finance loans are almost twice the loan recovery rates of comparable secured corporate loans, which average 45%. Over 50% of project finance loan recoveries are in the 90–100% range with a median of 92%, so it is effectively a barbell distribution with some lenders recovering close to 100% while other lenders recover minimal amounts.

Project finance characteristics that mitigate loss given default (LGD) and result in higher post-default loan recovery rates include:

Covenant and Security Package: Project finance lenders have a first-priority security interest in all project assets, shares, contracts, insurance policies, and cash flows. Allied to this, they also have a "step-in" regime (remedy, cure rights) pre-agreed with the project company's key project contract counterparties. This provides lenders with sufficient time to remedy a default (for example, replacing the project operator) and as a result, threshold covenants may be triggered before lenders incur any economic loss. Pre-agreed inter-creditor rights covering decision-making and voting rights in respect to enforcement and acceleration actions also serve to make the process more efficient.

Structural Mitigation: The legal sanctity of the senior secured preferred creditor status of project finance lenders—and the ringfenced/bankruptcy remote nature of the project SPV—helps to ensure that other creditors cannot emerge during bankruptcy proceedings, or the administrative process of project shareholders or related project parties, and attach claims against the project assets and contracts.

Strategic or Essential Nature of the Project: The robust nature of project finance structuring negotiations serves to achieve optimum stakeholder alignment and a balanced sharing of risk-adjusted returns across all stakeholders. The underlying philosophy that determines project success or not is essentially "If it's not fair, it's not sustainable." There are many examples of failed projects that can be traced back to an unequal or imbalanced sharing of the project economics among shareholders. Many people think that the financing is concluded at financial close when the reality is that financial close is just the beginning. For any project to overcome the unexpected economic events that will inevitably happen, there needs to be strong stakeholder interest alignment and a mutual incentive to find ways to ensure the project overcomes these external shocks. The commercial, economic, and strategic alignment that underpins the importance of a project ensures that project structures have built-in incentives for project stakeholders to mitigate economic loss.

GLOBAL INFRASTRUCTURE OUTLOOK

Infrastructure investment is a critical enabler of social and economic progress and development. The socioeconomic return on infrastructure investment is approximately 20% according to a June 2016 study by McKinsey Global Institute.[4] Thus, in effect, $1 of extra infrastructure investment increases gross domestic product (GDP) by 20 cents. The Asian Development Bank (ADB) arrived at a similar conclusion, determining that the elasticity of total output to infrastructure investment is 0.20–0.40.[5] Yet despite the overwhelming evidence that infrastructure investment is a positive catalyst for improved capital and labor mobility, as well as increased productivity and knowledge transfer within and across economies, emerging market countries in Asia and Latin America—as well as the developed economies of the US and Europe—show a widening gap between actual, current infrastructure spending and infrastructure needs. Several industry estimates suggest that the global investment spend on infrastructure is approximately $2.5 billion per annum versus the $3.5–3.7 billion per annum estimated to be required to support and underpin current and projected economic growth.

The Global Infrastructure Hub estimates infrastructure needs at $94 trillion between 2016 and 2040, or $3.7 trillion per year, equivalent to the annual GDP of Germany.[6] This is 19% or about $18 trillion higher than current infrastructure spending trends. Globally, we are currently allocating about 2.5–3% of GDP toward infrastructure spending when we need to be allocating 3.4–3.7% of GDP to meet future economic growth. Meeting the UN's Sustainable Development Goals (SDG's) for drinking water, sanitation, and access to electricity will require a further $3.5 trillion of infrastructure investment by 2030.[7] Asian economies represent the greatest infrastructure investment requirements from 2016–2040 at over 54%, of which China is 30% or $28 trillion of the total.

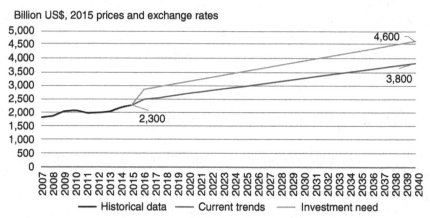

Source: Global Infrastructure Hub, Global Infrastructure Outlook, Global Infrastructure Hub, Global Infrastructure Outlook, (Global Infrastructure Hub and Oxford Economics 2017).

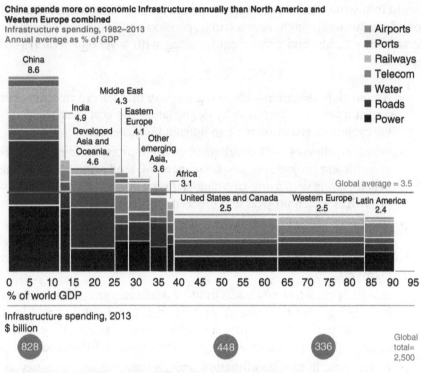

China spends more on economic infrastructure annually than North America and Western Europe combined
Infrastructure spending, 1982–2013
Annual average as % of GDP

■ Airports
■ Ports
▨ Railways
■ Telecom
■ Water
■ Roads
■ Power

China
8.6

Middle East
4.3

India
4.9

Eastern
Europe
4.1

Developed
Asia and
Oceania,
4.6

Other
emerging
Asia,
3.6

Africa
3.1

Global average = 3.5

United States and Canada
2.5

Western Europe
2.5

Latin America
2.4

0 5 10 15 20 25 30 35 40 45 50 55 60 65 70 75 80 85 90 95
% of world GDP

Infrastructure spending, 2013
$ billion

828   448   336

Global
total=
2,500

1. Percentage of world GDP generated by the 75 countries in our analysis for 2013.
2. Includes Australia, Hong Kong, Japan, New Zealand, and Singapore.
3. Includes Bangladesh, Indonesia, Malaysia, Pakistan, Philippines, Sri Lanka, Taiwan, Thailand, and Vietnam.

Source: McKinsey Global Institute, Bridging Global Infrastructure Gaps.

While Asia and particularly China have the largest infrastructure needs, these economies are outspending the rest of the world; Asia is investing on average about 5% of GDP on infrastructure compared to 2.5% in the case of US, Europe, and Latin America. In fact, China spends more on infrastructure as a percent of GDP than the United States, Canada, and Western Europe combined.[8]

A major cause for the widening infrastructure gap in emerging markets is increases in public debt to GDP, which constrains public financing options, while many Western economies have significantly reduced infrastructure spending due to fiscal austerity following the 2008 financial crisis. Measures that could increase the flow of private sector institutional investor capital toward infrastructure investment and unlock part of the estimated $120 trillion of institutional capital across banks, pension and insurance companies, infrastrucure funds, and private equity along with sovereign wealth funds include:

- Accounting treatment—changing the way that governments account for infrastructure spending by depreciating the cost over the project life cycle versus incurring as an upfront budget expense;
- Better pipeline of well developed/bankable projects—more effective and efficient project selection/management, land acquisition/permits in place along with a one-stop shop national infrastructure agency that prioritizes which projects will proceed;
- Improved risk-adjusted returns for investors—many projects are awarded based on lowest construction cost bids versus total life cycle costs. Ultimately cost overruns are passed on to, and borne by, taxpayers;
- Bundling infrastructure assets to address transaction costs and illiquidity. There is pent-up demand on the part of pension funds and insurance companies for infrastrucure investment assets as they provide optimal alignment and matching of assets and liabilities; and
- Better cross-border coordination and real market transperancy and standarization.

THE INFRASTRUCTURE GAP IN EMERGING MARKETS

Emerging markets will constitute an increasingly larger share of the global infrastructure market as economic growth shifts from slower growth developed markets to faster growing emerging markets. Global challenges such as population growth, urbanization, and climate change are accelerating the critical need for infrastructure investment in emerging markets. Two-thirds of the estimated $69 trillion of global infrastructure investment needs from 2017–2035 will come from emerging markets with Asia constituting 54% and China and India combined representing 42%.[9] McKinsey notes that at the current rate of infrastructure investment spending, the shortfall or gap in infrastructure spending will be 11% or $350 billion per year.

Government debt has increased over the last ten years, with average debt-to-GDP levels for developing countries approaching and exceeding 50%—debt levels not seen since the 1980s. These fiscal constraints on government spending have led to declining public spending on infrastructure and exacerbated the infrastructure spending gap.

FOCUS—ASIA INFRASTRUCTURE NEEDS

Infrastructure is a critical catalyst for reducing poverty, driving economic growth, and improving quality of life. Despite significant infrastructure investment in Asia, the continent still has over 400 million people with no access to electricity, 300 million with no access to safe drinking water, and 1.5 billion people lacking basic sanitation. In 2009, the Asia Development Bank (ADB) produced a report analyzing infrastructure investment (defined as transport, power, telecommunications, and sanitation) requirements for developing Asia in 2010–2020.[10] The study covered 35 of the 45 Asian developing member countries (DMCs) and covered four sectors: electricity, transportation, telecommunications, and water and sanitation. The report estimated that total infrastructure investment needs (the gap between current infrastructure investment spend and projected needs) between 2009 and 2020 would be slightly less than $8 trillion or about $750 billion per year.

In 2016, the ADB updated its 2009 report for the period 2016–2030 and significantly increased the estimation of infrastructure needs in Asia to $22 trillion or $1.5 trillion per year—effectively a 100% increase from the $750 billion per year estimate in 2009.[11] This was based on an assumption that economic growth would range from 3% to 7% across Asia. In terms of GDP spend, the $22 trillion of projected infrastructure needs represents 2.4% per annum of Asia's annual GDP—5% when China is excluded. The ADB also studied the cost impact of climate change (cost of climate mitigation primarily related to greenhouse gas reduction in the power sector and climate-proofing transport infrastructure). The ADB estimated the incremental climate change investment costs were $4 trillion between 2016 and 2030, bringing the total infrastructure investment needs for Asia to a staggering $26 trillion or $1.7 trillion per year for the region. East Asia (primarily China) accounts for 60% of the $26 trillion investment need while power and transporation represent over 80%. Asia currently invests $880 billion per year on infrastrcuture, resulting in an infrastructure gap of 50% or 2.4% of annual GDP (5% when China is excluded). While China has been one of the largest infrastructure investors in the world (spending around 8–10% of annual GDP over the last decade), it still has a long way to go to close the gap with developed countries in terms of the level or stock and quality of infrastructure. For example, the stock of road transport infrastructure in China is $283 million per square km. This compares with $1.275 billion per square km in OECD countries.

The ADB report highlights the escalating challenge of meeting the growing infrastrucuture needs of the 45 countries comprising developing Asia, which will reach $22 trillion (factoring in climate change mitigation increases the infrastructure gap to over $26 trillion) over the next 15 years according to the ADB. The scale of the numbers should serve as a rallying call to mobilize and prioritize both private and public sector support for infrastructure investment solutions. The solutions required to close the infrastructure gap in Asia will be many and varied, from unlocking private sector finance and investment in infrastructure to public sector tax and spending reforms while maintaining public debt sustainability. Equally important, the public sector needs to establish robust regulatory frameworks to encourage private sector investment and participation in infrastructure.

ENDNOTES

1. Benjamin Esty, *The Economic Motivations for Using Project Finance* (Harvard Business School, 2002).
2. Refinitiv, *Global Project Finance Review* (Full Year 2019), 2.
3. S&P Global Market Intelligence, *Annual Global Project Finance Default and Recovery Study, 1980–2014* (S&P Global Market Intelligence, 2016).
4. McKinsey Global Institute, *Bridging Global Infrastructure Gaps* (McKinsey & Company 2016).
5. Asian Development Bank, *Meeting Asia's Infrastructure Needs* (ADB 2017) Manila. © ADB. https://www.adb.org/publications/asia-infrastructure-needs.
6. Global Infrastructure Hub, *Global Infrastructure Outlook* (Global Infrastructure Hub and Oxford Economics 2017). Licensed from the Global Infrastructure Hub Ltd under a Creative Commons Attribution 3.0 Australia License. To the extent permitted by law, the GI Hub disclaims liability to any person or organization in respect of anything done, or omitted to be done, in reliance upon information contained in this publication.
7. Global Infrastructure Hub, *Global Infrastructure Outlook* (Global Infrastructure Hub and Oxford Economics 2017).
8. McKinsey Global Institute, *Bridging Global Infrastructure Gaps.*

9. McKinsey Global Institute, *Bridging Global Infrastructure Gaps: Has the World Made Progress* (McKinsey & Company 2017).

10. Asian Development Bank, "Infrastructure for a Seamless Asia" (ADB 2009) Manila. © ADB. https://www.adb.org/sites/default/files/publication/159348/adbi-infrastructure-seamless-asia.pdf.

11. Asian Development Bank, *Meeting Asia's Infrastructure Needs* (ADB 2017) Manila. © ADB. https://www.adb.org/publications/asia-infrastructure-needs.

CHAPTER 2

Project Finance—Risk Analysis and Mitigation

Risk analysis and mitigation is one of the key lynchpins and critical skill sets of project finance. The risk analysis and mitigation methodology can be summarized by the acronym IAMA—Identify, Assess, Mitigate or Allocate. The guiding principle and approach to project finance risk mitigation is to allocate project finance risks to those project parties best able to bear them such that the residual risks that remain with the project company borrower are manageable and acceptable. The objective is to allocate away project risks to project stakeholders (project sponsors, construction contractor, operator, government, etc.) such that the project borrower retains sufficient but not excessive risks. Retain too many risks and the project will not be sustainable and will fail, while allocating too many risks to project parties will increase the required adjusted risk returns those parties will require. Another method to address project risks is to mitigate via insurance cover, contingent lending (e.g., cost overrun loans), or changes to project contracts. While many financial disciplines involve risk analysis and mitigation, project finance is unique in using contractual risk mitigation to achieve optimal identification and allocation of all project risks to those parties best able to bear them, such that the project achieves the optimal risk/return for all project stakeholders. This ensures the project is sustainable and able to absorb all future risk events, and relevant stakeholders are incentivized to ensure the project risk events are mitigated. The project company operates at the center of an extensive network of contractual relationships that attempt to allocate a variety of project risks to those parties best suited to appraise and control them via contracts (project finance = contract financing). For example, construction risk is typically borne by the construction contractor and the risk of insufficient demand for the project output by the project offtaker.

Project Risk Overview

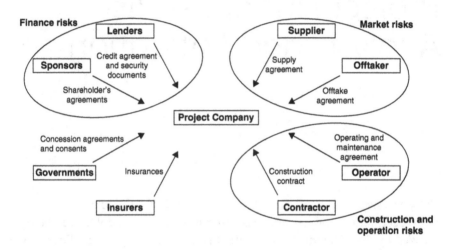

One of the biggest potential errors in structuring and negotiating project finance deals is for one or more stakeholders to secure a disproportionate share of the project economics such that the risk/return trade-off is unbalanced. As a financial advisor or structuring bank, the key is to ensure a fair and equitable allocation of risks and project returns such that there is an optimal alignment of commercial and financial interests that ensures project sustainability. For many of the project finance deals that have failed, it has been largely down to misalignment of risk/return when projects have encountered negative external risk events. It is important to always keep in mind that project finance borrowers are highly leveraged, thinly capitalized start-up SPVs that have no revenues and cash flows and typically have considerable construction risk. One of the takeaways after 20 years structuring and executing project finance deals is that the project deal does not end at financial close—it begins at financial close when the assumptions that form the basis of the project are tested by unforeseen and unexpected risk events.

Project finance risks can be largely grouped into three categories: (1) commercial risks (project risks inherent to project finance such as basic commercial viability, construction, operation, input/feedstock, revenue, and environmental risks); (2) macroeconomic or financial risks (external macroeconomic events such as inflation, foreign exchange, and interest rate risk); and (3) regulatory and political risks (change in law or adverse government action or political force majeure, war/riots, expropriation, currency convertibility/transfer). The following sections cover the key categories of commercial risks, macroeconomic risks, and political and regulatory risks.

COMMERCIAL VERSUS CONTRACT VIABILITY

One of the first and most important steps in assessing the financial feasibility of a potential project finance transaction is to ask macro questions regarding the fundamental need and commercial rationale for the project. Questions such as: Is there a sound and sustainable market for the product that the project will produce absent the long-term offtake or revenue contract? Is the project cost competitive? Is the price reasonable? Do end users or offtakers have the willingness and ability to pay for the project production? While most project finance deals have revenue offtake contracts for a sufficient tenor to match the loan tenor with a slight "contract tail" (typically 2–3 years), it is important to "look through" the contractual framework to understand if the project is still commercially viable should the project contracts fall away. Another key related issue is the dependence on third parties (local, state, or governmental entities) for critical infrastructure to facilitate project completion. For example, a transmission line or pipeline interconnection may be required to allow a power plant to perform construction completion tests and commence commercial operations. While the timely completion of this related project infrastructure may be the obligation of a third party, it is important to ensure that the revenue offtake contract becomes effective and the offtake payment obligations are triggered even if third-party infrastructure is not completed.

SPONSOR RISK

While project finance is routinely referred to as non-recourse financing, there will invariably be certain project risks that the project sponsor will be required to assume. So more correctly, project finance is a form of limited recourse financing. In most cases project sponsors are typically required to provide some level of project construction completion support—usually capped by amount and time. This form of sponsor support can take the form of contingent equity, a cost overrun guarantee, or a full completion guarantee. Sponsor limited recourse support can also take the form of guarantees in relation to the revenue offtake contract and typically consists of price floor support on commodity risk projects or a limited cash flow deficiency guarantee. Project sponsor risk analysis also involves an assessment of the experience and creditworthiness of the project sponsor in relation to the specific project undertaking. Key questions to ask include:

1. Does the sponsor have a successful track record of constructing and implementing projects of this scale, size, technology, and nature?

2. Does the sponsor possess the resources and expertise to oversee and monitor the EPC contract?

3. Does the sponsor have the financial strength to stand behind the various project guarantees and undertakings? Ideally lenders require a minimum single A credit rating from sponsors or absent this, some form of credit enhancement such as a bank letter of credit or surety bond.

4. Does the sponsor have the committed ability to subscribe the required equity investment? Lenders may require financially weaker sponsors to either subscribe the equity investment upfront before the debt is disbursed or "commit" the equity via a bank letter of credit or parent company guarantee.

5. Does the project represent a material percentage of the sponsor's assets or revenues? If the project represents a significant percentage (over 20%) of assets and/or revenues, then that is a red flag.

6. Is the project integral and strategic to the sponsor's core business activities such that they have a strong incentive to stand behind and support the project? What we sometimes refer to as "walk away risk."

In projects involving smaller and financially weaker sponsors, the mitigation of direct financial risk (equity committed/subscribed upfront, no recourse guarantees or financial dependence on sponsor) and sole reliance on sponsor project management and operational expertise may appear acceptable. However, there have been cases where projects have failed due to unrelated financial issues with other operational or business activities of the sponsor or corporate-level financial problems that resulted in a risk contagion effect between sponsor risk and project risk, ultimately causing the project to fail. Therefore, it is critical to conduct comprehensive due diligence on the sponsor and to ensure one fully understands the entire commercial and financial activities of the sponsor and related and unrelated third parties. It is sometimes not possible to completely insulate and ring fence the project from contamination risk of the sponsor.

POLITICAL RISK

Political risk is one of the most challenging risk issues affecting project finance transactions in developing countries. Infrastructure projects are long-lived assets that typically transcend political events and changes of government in the country concerned.

Political risks can be broken down into three broad categories:

- **political unrest and war/riots;**
- **nationalization/expropriation; and**
- **currency convertibility/transfer.**

It is difficult or impossible to predict and anticipate when or if a "triggering event" might occur that could result in a political risk event. Triggering events can vary from small/incremental policy changes (such as change in law or taxes) that are discriminatory and can eventually result in an expropriation event (referred to as "creeping expropriation") or outright insurrection, war, riots, or terrorism. Political risk affects investors and lenders alike. Mitigation measures include explicit political risk insurance (PRI) policies covering either or both the sponsors' equity investment and the lenders' loan exposure and/or implicit PRI cover by having multi-lateral development banks (MDBs) such as the International Finance Corporation (IFC), the ADB, or the Inter-American Development Bank (IDB Invest) provide direct lending to the project. MDBs benefit from special status as preferred creditors (priority access to foreign exchange, waiver from government capital controls, exclusion from sovereign debt reschedule/restructuring, sovereign bilateral lending relationships) that is effectively transferred or bestowed on the project deal by virtue of their lending to the project. This political risk mitigation effect is commonly referred to as the "halo effect," which serves to mitigate adverse sovereign actions that could negatively affect the project.

The relevant impact of the three categories of political risks varies depending on the location and underlying nature of the infrastructure project in question. For example, power projects that typically generate local currency revenues are more susceptible to currency convertibility/transfer risks due to the need to convert and transfer local currency into foreign currency and remit offshore to repay loan obligations. The 1997 Asian currency crisis laid bare this risk when several Asian countries' currency pegs to the USD collapsed, precipitating capital controls, currency mismatch, and inability to convert and transfer sufficient offshore currency. The Argentina financial crisis and resulting currency peg collapse of 2001 also resulted in large political risk insurance claims by project deals for currency convertibility/transfer events, which resulted in project loan defaults. Unlike power projects or local currency infrastructure projects in emerging markets, natural resource projects (mining or oil and gas projects) are less susceptible to currency risks as the output from natural resource projects is typically designated for export with the revenue proceeds remitted by the offtaker in USD into offshore bank accounts controlled by the lenders. Expropriation/nationalization risk is also generally reduced for some natural resource projects where "diversion risk" is low (e.g., the government lacks the expertise to operate the project or does not have access to critical feedstock supplies). That said, oil and gas projects can be more susceptible to expropriation/nationalization risk given the politicized nature of domestic resources viewed as being sovereign assets of the state and strong cash flows of these projects. Venezuela is a good example of "creeping expropriation" leading to full-scale expropriation/nationalization of oil and gas projects. In 2001, the Chaves administration introduced a tax reform law that doubled the royalty payments from 16.6% to 30% and required state oil company PDVSA to have a majority ownership interest (from 20% minority ownership at the time) in foreign-owned oil and gas projects. This form of escalating or creeping expropriation eventually resulted in foreign oil and gas investors surrendering their investments to Venezuela and leaving the country, effectively resulting in a re-nationalization of the oil and gas sector.

CONSTRUCTION AND COMPLETION RISK

Infrastructure projects typically entail large/complex construction risks with the construction period varying from 3 years for power projects to 4–5 years for large-scale liquefied natural gas (LNG) projects, refinery, and certain mining and commodity processing/petrochemical projects. The inherent construction risks leading to potential cost overruns and delays as well as shortfalls in project performance upon completion makes construction risk one of the major contributors to project finance default rates during the construction period and initial ramp-up period postconstruction completion. According to S&P, 75% of all project finance loan defaults occur in the first 3–5 years of the project life cycle when construction/completion and start-up risk is most acute.[1] Construction risk mitigation measures include fixed price, date-certain turnkey EPC contracts (which substantially transfers construction risk to the construction contractor), the inclusion of construction cost overrun contingencies in project costs (market norm is 10% total EPC costs or approximately 7–8% of total project costs), limited (capped by time and amount) sponsor completion support, or inclusion of a separate/stand-alone cost overrun standby loan facility. Fossil fuel–fired power projects and certain processing projects (petrochemical, refineries, oil/gas pipelines, etc.) generally have fixed price, date-certain turnkey EPC contracts. It is difficult and/or cost prohibitive to secure turnkey EPC contracts for projects that entail a large civil works component and have subsurface, geotechnical, or ground risks as is the case with hydroelectric power projects, oil and gas, and mining projects. These projects usually require full sponsor completion recourse guarantees by project finance lenders.

Site Acquisition, Access, and Permits

Project permits, rights of way, and so forth, required to acquire or access the site of the project are usually borne by the EPC contractor or the relevant government or municipal agency. This pre-construction risk is often overlooked and can be highly problematic for pipeline and transmission line projects requiring rights of way and permits across large land tracts. In some emerging markets where land title laws are not well defined, this can prove to be a complicated and protracted process. It is more usual to pass this risk on to the relevant local or central government authority to secure the necessary project permits and rights of way as a precondition to issuing the Notice to Proceed (NTP) to the EPC contractor to start construction.

EPC Contractor

The experience and track record of the EPC contractor is a critical lender consideration when evaluating construction risk. The EPC contractor should have recent and relevant experience with the project in question and a solid track record of completing these projects on schedule and within budget. Relevant knowledge and experience with any underlying technology being used in the project as well as experience in the country where the project is being implemented are also critical. Lenders may also raise concerns if the size of the project is relevant to the size of total revenues of the EPC company—typically lenders would not want the project to represent more than 10–15% of the EPC contractor's total revenues. The financial strength and creditworthiness of the EPC company is also important as the EPC company will typically have to provide financial guarantees/surety bonds to backstop the completion and performance guarantee undertakings contained in the EPC contract. A minimum credit rating of single A is generally required by lenders by the EPC company; if this condition is not met, lenders require the EPC company to post standby letters of credit or surety bond issued by a minimum single A rated commercial bank.

Construction Cost Overrun/Delay in Completion

There are three significant effects from unexpected delays in construction completion: loss of project revenues, potential penalties due to the offtaker, and increased interest during construction (IDC) on project debt outstanding. EPC contracts will typically contain penalties or LDs for construction delays due to the fault of the EPC contractor. These LDs are expressed as payments per each day of delay and are typically capped at around 15–20% of the total EPC contract price and sized to cover roughly 6 months of lost project revenues, penalties due to the offtaker, IDC, and so forth. Lenders should ensure there are minimal carve-outs in the EPC contract for delays due to change in scope of the project, change orders, site condition, change in law, and so forth. At a minimum, any of these carve-outs in the EPC contract should be mirrored or passed through to the offtaker in the offtake contract. Project finance lenders should also seek to negotiate tight construction completion criteria in the EPC contract while keeping completion undertakings as loose/flexible as possible in the corresponding offtake contract to minimize potential negative financial impact on the project company.

Inadequate Performance Upon Completion

EPC performance delays arise when the guaranteed performance criteria in the EPC contract fails to be achieved upon project completion. Before handover between the EPC contractor and the project owner and before the EPC contractor is released from their construction contract obligations, a performance test (overseen by the lenders' independent engineer, or IE) will be undertaken to demonstrate the project's ability to meet the minimum performance and operational requirements in the offtake contract and the technical assumptions reflected in the lenders' base-case financial model.

The performance test protocol varies depending on the industrial sector and the underlying technology risk; however, it is typical for lenders to require a 90-day performance test protocol, which the lenders' IE will sign off before final physical construction completion is deemed to be achieved. Lenders also sometimes require a further "financial" completion test to demonstrate a project's ability to generate revenues and offtaker's ability and willingness to pay. For example, lenders might require 6 months of operational performance and achievement of a minimum DSCR per base-case financial model before the full physical and financial completion is deemed to have occurred and any supporting completion guarantees fall away.

Fixed price, turnkey EPC contracts will usually contain performance penalties/LDs due from the EPC contractor to cover any performance shortfall. The performance LDs (as with delay LDs) are sized based on the IE's technical review of the project and estimate of a worst-case scenario. Performance LDs are typically 10% of the EPC contract price with total LDs for delay and performance capped at 25–30% of total EPC contract price. Performance LDs are typically structured as a debt buydown, where they are used to reduce outstanding debt to offset the project performance shortfall such that lenders' base-case DSCRs can be achieved. For example, if a power project was guaranteed to achieve a 90% plant capacity factor but could only achieve a maximum of 85% per the performance tests, the project would use the performance LDs to prepay a part of the project debt to offset the performance shortfall and lost revenues and any penalties due to the offtaker such that the original base-case DSCR is achieved.

OPERATION AND MAINTENANCE RISK

Operation and maintenance (O&M) risk relates to the project's capacity to operate at optimal design specifications consistent with the requirements of the offtake contract. As the lead project sponsor is likely to be a strategic investor (versus financial investor) with relevant industry experience operating similar projects, it is common for the project operator to be one of the project sponsors. This dual role of sponsor and operator creates a positive alignment of interests, which ensures the project will operate as expected. O&M risk is mitigated by the relative ease and ability to replace the project operator due to poor operational performance: for example, there are many utilities and IPP companies capable of operating power plants.

O&M contracts are either in the form of fixed-cost agreements or cost-plus agreements. Fixed-price contracts have the advantage of a predetermined fixed budget cost for operating the project while cost-plus contracts create more cost escalation risk for the project as costs are not capped while guaranteeing a profit margin to the operator. Including a penalty/bonus payment feature in the O&M contract serves to create incentives to optimize operational performance while constraining costs. If the operational budget can be determined with a high degree of accuracy, then a fixed-cost contract makes sense. The risk inherent in cost-plus contracts can be mitigated by having the lenders' IE review and approve the initial operational cost budget and allowing automatic annual approvals subject to the next annual operational budget being within ±10% of the prior annual budget cost. While instituting cost controls and requiring project lender approval for any major operational budgetary items is important, it is also critical that project operations are not unduly interrupted or impeded as this could trigger potential technical events of default under the offtake agreement. Additional contingencies to mitigate O&M risks include maintaining a 3- or 6-month O&M reserve account to be used for any O&M cost overruns. It is also typical to include a major maintenance reserve account funded from project cash flows to cover major maintenance costs for the project.

SUPPLY RISKS

Supply risks depend on the underlying nature of the project. Processing/tolling projects such as gas or oil pipelines, transmission lines, certain LNG, and petrochemical and refinery projects do not entail fuel or feedstock supply risks as they are simply contracted on an availability basis to provide transmission or transportation services or to toll/process commodities supplied or delivered by the owner/sponsor. Supply risk occurs in projects where there is a critical long-term fuel or feedstock supply contract entered into by the project. For example, a gas-fired power project with a 20-year offtake contract will require a matching gas supply contract for delivery of natural gas in the volumes and specifications required. Clearly, supplier reliability and consistent quality of supply is critical to the project. If the supply contract is on a take or pay basis, it is important to ensure that these supply costs can be fully passed through to the offtaker and that there is contract harmony between the supply contract and the offtake contract in relation to contract terms such as contract commencement date, termination events, and force majeure events: for example, if the offtaker is relieved from taking/buying electricity from the project due to a natural force majeure event, it is important that the project has matching force majeure relief from taking/buying natural gas under the gas supply contract.

To mitigate unexpected, short-term interruptions in supply, it is normal for projects to have a temporary backup fuel supply on site. For example, gas-fired power projects will typically have storage tanks containing 30–60-day diesel supplies to allow the power plant to continue operating in the event there is a natural gas supply interruption (for example, damage or a problem with the gas pipeline). Supply risks can also be covered by obtaining natural force majeure insurance cover or business interruption insurance cover as part of the project insurance package.

RESERVE RISK

Oil and gas as well as mining projects, which entail the commercialization of finite, proven reserves, require lenders to assume reserve risk when lending: the risk the projected reserves do not materialize as expected. This form of lending is referred to as reserve-based lending (RBL) when used to finance oil and gas reserves. To protect against reserve risk, lenders will only provide financing against a discounted percentage of the proven and probable reserves as determined by a reservoir engineer acting on behalf of the lenders. Lenders will also require that a minimum "reserve tail" is maintained at all times—typically 30%—as an insurance buffer against reserve risk. The quantum of proven and probable reserves, the production curve, and oil price projections are re-determined every 6 months, and the borrowing base is effectively reset periodically. If the outstanding loans exceed the new/re-determined borrowing base, then there will be a required prepayment to bring the outstanding borrowings in line with the new borrowing base. Conversely, if the borrowing base exceeds the loan amount, then there is no requirement for prepayment. Mining projects do not incorporate a borrowing base formula reset periodically like oil and gas RBL; however, they do have reserve tail requirements and also additional forward-looking cash flow tests such as minimum loan life coverage ratio and project life coverage ratio tests.

SALES/OFFTAKE RISK

The offtake or revenue contract is the critical agreement in a project finance deal underpinning the revenues and cash flows required to cover project costs, service project debt, and provide an equity return to the sponsor investors. Project lenders will seek a sales/offtake contract that produces a stable and robust revenue stream such that volume and price risks are fully mitigated. There are four general sales/offtake contract structures in project finance depending on the nature and industry sector of the project as follows:

1. Take-or-Pay Contract

Take-or-pay contracts stipulate that the offtaker either must take the project production output or make a payment with respect to this production output. This contract structure is typically applied to power generation projects and effectively ensures a firm and stable revenue stream for the project such that volume and price risks are fully mitigated. For power deals, the offtake contract typically comprises a capacity payment and an energy payment, whereby the capacity payment is paid as long as the project is available to produce electricity and covers the project's capital costs including debt service, fixed operating expenses, and equity investment returns to shareholders. The energy payment is a variable payment paid by the offtaker whenever the project actually generates electricity and effectively covers the fuel cost as a pass-through cost to the offtaker as well as other variable operating costs. Take-or-pay contracts are the tightest form of offtake contract ensuring a firm, predictable, and stable revenue stream to the project.

2. Long-Term Sales Agreement

Long-term sales agreement offtake contracts are typically associated with oil and gas, mining, and petrochemical project financings, which entail commodity price market risk on the production output. Under this form of offtake contract, the production volume risk is assigned to the offtaker, who provides a minimum volume offtake commitment at the prevailing international market price for the commodity output in question. Project lenders will seek to mitigate and minimize commodity price risk as follows:

- Use conservative commodity price projections provided by the lenders' market consultant when designing the lenders' base-case financial model—including worse-case downside scenarios—to ensure project can withstand a protracted low commodity price environment;

- Ensure the project is a low-cost producer—ideally, lowest quartile on the industry cost curve;
- Adjust project leverage and target a minimum DSCR to reflect commodity price risk and potential cash flow volatility—ideally, a DSCR of 1.75–2.0x; and
- Seek to link or index commodity prices where there is a commodity input feedstock and a separate commodity output price to insulate the project from changes in commodity prices and ensure a firm operating cash flow margin—for example, an aluminum smelting project whose key feedstock supply is alumina might seek to structure the offtake contract to index or link the commodity price for alumina with the offtake market price for aluminum such that the alumina feedstock price rises and falls in line with the commodity price for the project output, aluminum.

3. Availability-Based Contracts

Availability-based contracts are used in conjunction with projects providing a processing service. Provided the project is available to operate per the offtake contract, the offtake payment must be made. Examples of the application of this contract form include gas pipelines and transmission lines that enter into gas transportation agreements and transmission line agreements, respectively, under which the project undertakes to transport natural gas or transmit electricity as and when directed. The entity contracting for these transport and transmission services is required to make a firm payment regardless of the quantum of natural gas or electricity transported or transmitted—so long as the project is "available" to provide these services. Projects that involve some form of processing service (referred to as tolling contracts) such as LNG regasification plants, also utilize this form of offtake contract structure.

Availability-based contracts provide a very stable, firm, and predicable revenue stream to the project and as such can support high leverage (80% and upward) and low required DSCRs (minimum of 1.20–1.25x).

4. Concession Contracts

Concession contracts are used for infrastructure projects such as toll roads, airports, ports, social infrastructure, and so forth, under which the project company is granted a fixed concession period (20–30 years) under which it is required to provide services meeting minimum performance standards. The concession granting authority is typically a public sector entity. Concession contracts entail usage risk for project finance lenders (traffic risk in case of, say, toll roads). Usage risk mitigation typically entails the use of traffic studies and government minimum revenue guarantees.

APPROVALS AND PERMITS

Ensuring that all required government and municipal approvals and permits are obtained and in full force and effect to allow the project to acquire the site and commence construction activities is an often overlooked project risk as a secondary order of importance by lenders. It is critical that all required approvals and permits are in place as a precondition to financial close. The obligation to ensure the approvals and permits are secured can either be allocated to the construction contractor or—as is more likely the case—to the relevant government authority. However, this may prove more challenging in emerging markets where the legal framework covering land ownership and title is less clearly defined and more problematic. Hence, executing some form of government support agreement to assist with securing the required approvals and permits will be important.

SOCIAL AND ENVIRONMENTAL CONSIDERATIONS

Social and environmental risks have become more acute concerns for project finance lenders, in particular commercial banks, in the last 10–15 years. The origins of this focus on social and environmental risks can be traced back to a number of highly problematic project financings in the early 2000s, which entailed significant negative social and environmental risk impacts. In particular, the 2001 $1.3 billion OCP pipeline project in Ecuador was a cautionary tale. OCP is a 300-mile oil pipeline project from the interior rain forests of Ecuador to the Pacific coast that traverses 11 ecosystems, 6 active volcanos, and numerous indigenous communities and has extensive biodiversity and endangered species impact issues. The project was strongly opposed by major international environmental groups and NGOs. A series of oil leaks precipitated a major backlash against the two financial institutions leading the $900 million project financing and resulted in significant reputational damage for lenders.

In the aftermath of OCP and a number of other project finance deals that had negative social and environmental impacts, commercial banks sought to implement formal principles and procedures for analyzing, assessing, and mitigating social and environmental risks. Out of this effort was born the Equator Principles (EPs) in 2003 with the original signatories comprising 6 banks.

The EPs are a voluntary set of standards that were developed by leading financial institutions in June 2003 with the objective of ensuring that projects are developed in a socially responsible manner reflecting sound environmental management practices. The EPs were based on existing environmental and social policy frameworks established by the IFC and essentially required EP member banks to follow a set of 10 principles commencing with initial project categorization: Category A representing a high or significant risk impact project, Category B a limited or moderate risk impact project, and Category C representing a minimal or no risk impact project. Category A and B projects required completion of an environmental impact assessment study and a resulting action and monitoring plan to mitigate social and environmental risks. This is conducted with the assistance of a social and environmental consultant retained by the lending banks. Banks are also required to report and disclose their EP-related lending activities, although NGOs and environmental groups have criticized the lack of detailed information in these reports as the data is high level and aggregated, and it is impossible to identify specific projects or to peer inside the decision-making black box of the banks in question.

EP is a risk management framework adopted by financial institutions for determining, assessing, and managing environmental and social risk in project finance. It is primarily intended to provide a minimum standard for due diligence to support responsible risk decision-making. As of May 2020, 104 financial institutions in 38 countries have officially adopted EP, covering the majority of international project finance debt in emerging and developed markets. The last iteration of the EPs (EP3) was adopted in June 2013 and expanded the scope of EPs to cover project finance advisory mandates, project finance–related corporate loans, and project finance bridge loans. EP4—among other things—expands the scope of transactions to include project finance refinancing and project-related acquisition financing; it was approved in late 2019 and will become effective in October 2020.

FINANCIAL RISKS

Financial risks relate to external macroeconomic events such as changes in interest rates, inflation, and foreign exchange risks. Interest rate risks arise because commercial banks lend on a variable interest rate basis using the London Interbank Offer Rate (LIBOR) as the funding basis; hence the need to protect the project company from changes in LIBOR.[2] This is accomplished by financial institutions (typically one or more of the project lenders) providing interest rate swaps under which the project company executes an International Swaps and Derivative Association (ISDA) to swap the floating rate interest rate for a fixed interest rate. If LIBOR is above the fixed rate, then the swap provider pays the project company the difference between the floating and fixed rates, while if LIBOR is below the fixed rate, the project company pays the swap providers the difference up to the fixed rate. This ensures the project company will never incur interest expenses above the swap fixed rate and eliminates interest rate risk. The relative sensitivity of project cash flows to changes in interest rates will dictate what percentage of total debt needs to be hedged for interest rate risk, but generally 60–70% of total debt is required by lenders to be hedged. Foreign exchange risks usually arise in connection with the construction contract whereby equipment may be procured in different currencies, whose changes could negatively affect project costs. The risk is usually minimal given most project costs are USD denominated; however, if there are large equipment item costs, it is typically to try to enter into forward FX contracts for the construction period to lock in or fix the FX rate. Inflation risks are mitigated by including inflation indexing in offtake revenue contracts and harmonizing inflation indexing across all key project contracts.

FORCE MAJEURE RISK

Force majeure (FM) refers to unforeseen and unavoidable events beyond the control of the affected project contract counterparty that impedes or prevents the ability of said contract counterparty from performing under the contract. FM events are either natural FM events (accidents, floods, hurricanes, etc., considered acts of god) or political FM events (war, riots, civil unrest, changes in law/regulation, strikes). As FM events provide contract performance relief to the affected party, it is important to ensure that the definitions of FM are consistent and harmonized across all project agreements: for example, lenders would not want a power purchaser to have FM relief if under the fuel supply agreement, it is not an FM event, and thus the project is not relieved from continuing to purchase and pay for fuel.

Lenders can purchase private insurance cover for natural FM events to mitigate this risk while political FM risk is typically allocated to the government, who are the party best able to manage this risk. Delays in construction completion caused by FM can be insured against by purchasing delay in start-up (DSU) insurance, and FM events causing project operations to be affected can also be insured against by purchasing business interruption (BI) insurance. It is important to note that DSU and BI insurance only covers lost revenues/profits due to an insurable event causing actual physical damage to the project; it does not cover non-project physical damage events that cause the project to be affected. For example, a port strike that disrupts the import of construction equipment and delays construction would not typically be covered under DSU, nor would damage to a transmission line connecting the project to the electric grid or a gas pipeline interconnection supplying fuel to the project.

Project finance contracts distinguish between temporary and permanent FM events. Generally, FM relief is provided to address temporary, short-term, and unforeseen events that prevent one project party from performing. If the FM event continues beyond, say, 180 days, then it is usually considered to be a permanent FM event, and either project contract party would have the right to terminate the contract.

Case Study: Mozal Aluminum Project, Mozambique[3]

The Mozal Aluminum Project represents a good example of a successful project financing in a high-risk emerging market where project finance structuring is used to de-risk the financing. It is also an excellent example of how project financing and structural risk mitigation address "the paradox of infrastructure investment." The paradox of infrastructure investment provides that debt and equity investors require higher adjusted returns to compensate for project risks in high-risk emerging markets involving significant political risks, thus requiring the project generate material cash flows to meet the high returns demanded and in turn exposing the project to greater risk of adverse government action to expropriate and/or divert these cash flow streams. As a result, the project is exposed to greater risks. Project finance risk mitigation structuring techniques serve to reduce project risks and the associated required adjusted returns by investors and thus reduce the risk of adverse government actions against projects.

(continued)

(*continued*)

Project Overview and Background

Mozal is a $1.4 billion, 250,000-ton, large-scale aluminum smelter project in Mozambique. The project was conceived in the mid-1990s by a consortium comprising Gencor, the world's fourth-largest aluminum company at the time; South African development bank Industrial Development Corporation (IDC); along with Eskom, South Africa's integrated electric utility. The smelting technology would be supplied by French company Pechiney. Mozambique, a former Portuguese colony, achieved independence in 1975 and had just emerged from a 17-year civil war in 1992. By most international metrics, Mozambique was one of the poorest and most highly indebted countries in the world with a debt-to-GDP ratio of over 355% and GDP per capita of $50. Infrastructure had been decimated during the civil war along with critical legal and institutional frameworks, making it one of the highest political risk countries in the world at the time.

The project sponsors had just completed construction of a comparable 250,000-ton greenfield aluminum smelter called Hillside in South Africa in 1996 and were invited by the newly elected Mozambique government to build a similar project near Maputo in Mozambique. Gencor saw Mozambique as offering low-cost hydroelectric power—power is a critical input cost for aluminum smelting (25% of operating costs)—while Eskom viewed the project as an entry to Mozambique's electricity sector, which possessed significant hydroelectric potential and required massive investment to repair infrastructure damaged during the civil war. For Mozambique, the project would provide critical tax and royalty revenues while also being a catalyst for opening the country up to foreign direct investment (FDI). One of the key challenges faced by the project developers—aside from the political risk—was the relative materiality of the project given the Mozal project would equate to close to 100% of Mozambique's GDP, over 60% of the country's export revenues, and project output would be 13% of annual GDP at peak production.

Mozal Project Finance Risk Mitigation

The structural risk mitigation applied to Mozal served to materially de-risk the project as follows:

- *Construction Risk*—Mitigated as follows:
  - Project sponsors provided full completion guarantees;
  - Project cost overrun contingencies; and
  - Proven technology and synergies of Hillside smelter construction completed under budget and ahead of schedule using the same design technology and experienced construction companies.
- *Revenue Risk*—Mitigated as follows:
  - Mozal is a low-cost producer on the lowest quartile of the global cost curve of aluminum smelters due to cheap hydroelectric power and competitive alumina feedstock; and
  - Indexing of alumina feedstock cost to aluminum market price served to preserve a firm cash flow margin to the project and mitigate commodity price risk.
  - Financial Structure – Conservative
  - Low leverage (50%) and robust minimum DSCR of 2.0x; and
  - Inclusion of $150 million of subordinated debt representing 25% of total equity investment. The subordinated debt was "deep and dark" with a back-ended amortization and contained a PIK feature, which allowed for interest expense to be deferred during a downside aluminum price environment.
- *Political Risk*—Mitigated as follows:
  - Multi-sourced financing comprising the IFC, Export Credit Agencies (Coface of France, EDC of Canada, JBIC of Japan), and development banks (CDC of UK, DEG of Germany, and the European Investment Bank, or EIB) materially reduced political risks;
  - Role of IFC as an "honest broker" in structuring the project contracts, mediating negotiations between the government of Mozambique and the project sponsors helped ensure an alignment of interests across all stakeholders. Cross default between IFC and World Bank as major sovereign creditor

(continued)

(*continued*)

> to Mozambique further served to mitigate potential adverse government actions;
>
> - IFC provision of both senior debt and subordinated debt provided a "stamp of approval" on the project and helped catalyze other lenders to participate in the financing;
> - Low diversion risk as Mozambique has no alumina reserves. The value of tax and royalty revenues along with job creation and export proceeds and GDP growth also deters adverse sovereign actions; and
> - Government of Mozambique 4% equity ownership interest in Mozal.

Mozal Project Outcomes

The project sponsors elected to commence construction in 1998 before financial close using equity capital on the basis that the financing process was well advanced, and there was a high degree of confidence financial close would be achieved. Financial close subsequently followed in 1999, and construction was completed in 2000, ahead of schedule and $120 million under budget. The $680 million multi-source finance plan comprised the IFC, IDC, Coface, and ECA cover from the South African ECA CGIC. Mozal created 5,000 jobs during construction and 873 permanent jobs. Mozal also delivered significant positive macroeconomic outcomes for Mozambique: a 9% increase in Mozambique's annual GDP, an increase in exports by over $ 430 Million, which is 53% of total exports, and higher net foreign currency earnings of over $160 million. In 2003 the original financing was upsized and expanded to $1 billion to accommodate a doubling of Mozal's plant capacity from 250,000 tons to 500,000 tons and comprised a broader set of multilateral and bilateral development banks and lending institutions, including the addition of the Japanese and Canadian ECAs along with the German (DEG) and UK (CDC) bilateral development banks. This clearly demonstrates the ability of the IFC in acting as the "lender of last resort" to be a catalyst to mobilize private sector capital in high-risk emerging markets. Mozal Phase 2 construction completion was achieved in 2005 under budget and ahead of schedule. Mozal was a landmark infrastructure investment for Mozambique, which heralded the beginning of a pipeline of major infrastructure investments in the country. It also created a paradigm for a legal and regulatory framework, which served as a model for follow-on infrastructure and foreign direct investment. Most importantly, Mozal is an excellent example of how project finance structural risk mitigation can achieve superior and sustainable financial outcomes for all project stakeholders and avoid the paradox of infrastructure investment in emerging markets with material country risk.

ENDNOTES

1. S&P Global Market Intelligence, *Annual Global Project Finance Default and Recovery Study*.
2. The US funding and credit markets are currently in the midst of transitioning to using alternative benchmarks to LIBOR with the Federal Reserve Bank of New York advocating the Secured Overnight Financing Rate (https://www.newyorkfed.org/arrc/sofr-transition) from 2022 onward.
3. Benjamin Esty, *Financing the Mozal Project* (Harvard Business School, April 15, 2003).

CHAPTER 3

Project Finance Agreements and Loan Documentation

Project finance is also referred to as "contract financing," where the project company sits at the center of a series of project finance contracts and agreements. The project company is walled off as a legally independent special purpose company (SPC) or SPV established for the sole purpose of developing, owning, financing, constructing, and operating the underlying infrastructure project. The project company is the project contract counterparty for all key project contracts and agreements executed with various project stakeholders, including the construction contracts, operation contracts, input/feedstock and revenue offtake agreements, finance, and equity investment agreements, as well as any host government agreements.

Project Finance Contract Structure

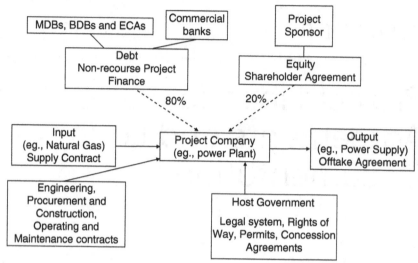

The project company is restricted from engaging in any business activities other than the specific infrastructure investment and is ring-fenced and "bankruptcy-remote" from the business activities of the owners and other project counterparties and tightly controlled by the project lenders. The lenders hold a perfected security interest over all project assets, including first lien mortgages over physical project assets, pledges/assignment of project agreements, insurances, cash flows, and the equity owners' shares in the project company. To maintain the sanctity of bankruptcy-remoteness, the legal and governance structure, decision-making, and operational and financing activities of the project company must be kept distinct and separate from those of the project sponsors and other related project parties.

Given the inter-connectivity and inter-dependence of the project agreements that make up the project finance transaction, it is critical that the project agreements are seamless and harmonized and that there are no contract mismatches. For example, it is important to ensure that FM provisions are harmonized across all agreements to avoid scenarios where the project company provides performance relief to, say, the fuel supplier for a fuel supply FM event while at the same time is not able to obtain FM performance relief from the offtaker. Similarly, the provisions dealing with LD penalties need to be consistent across contracts; for example, the LDs and penalties for project delay that the project company incurs under the offtake contract should be covered by the LD penalties payable by the construction contractor. Contract mismatch issues can also arise between the construction contract and the offtake agreement in relation to change in law, change orders, and guaranteed completion dates—it is important to ensure that these agreements are drafted to avoid any gaps or misalignment that might expose the project company to these contract mismatch risks.

CONSTRUCTION CONTRACTS IN PROJECT FINANCE

Project lenders ideally strive to allocate construction risk to the construction contractor via a fixed-price, date-certain turnkey EPC contract with LDs for construction completion delay and performance shortfall. While the EPC contractor will enter into subcontracts with other construction companies, it is important that the EPC contractor remains the single point of responsibility with the project company for the entire EPC contract. This is to avoid the risk of finger-pointing between the main contractor and the subcontractors if a problem should arise. The EPC contractor will build in the cost of providing a fully wrapped, turnkey EPC contract into the price of the construction contract. It is therefore not unusual for the project sponsors to decide to provide a completion guarantee in lieu of the more expensive turnkey EPC contract and seek to manage the construction risk and associated contracts in a more cost competitive way. For certain projects such as mining and hydroelectric power projects, which entail significant civil works along with sub-surface ground and seismic/geotechnical risks, it is more challenging to find EPC contractors willing to provide fully wrapped fixed price, date-certain EPC contracts. This is because construction companies are very reluctant to assume the sub-surface risks as they are not quantifiable. As such, project lenders will generally require the project sponsors to provide full recourse completion guarantees to cover the construction risks. One of the most heavily negotiated terms in the construction contract is the performance test protocol, which determines when/if the EPC contractor's obligations are satisfied and the project company assumes title and ownership to the project and also when/if any sponsor completion guarantee support is released. Construction completion performance tests vary from project to project depending on the industrial sector and whether technology is proven or unproven but are typically 60–90 days in duration and seek to substantiate the project's ability to perform under a variety of operational conditions. The lenders' IE will typically monitor the completion tests and provide sign-off to the lenders that the tests have been satisfactorily completed.

OPERATIONS AND MAINTENANCE CONTRACTS IN PROJECT FINANCE

The operator of the project enters into an operations and maintenance (O&M) agreement, which sets forth the operational obligations of the operator, including minimum operational performance requirements—generally to operate in line with industry standards—maintain operations manuals and health and safety and personnel records, ensure proper maintenance and inspections, and keep operational costs within pre-agreed budgets. Given the operator is required to have relevant industry experience and expertise operating similar projects and technologies, it is typically the case that one of the strategic project sponsors will also act as the project operator. This dual role creates a positive alignment of interests as the project sponsor has an added incentive to ensure the project is operated to achieve optimal operational performance.

O&M contract structures consist of three main formats: (1) fixed-cost O&M contract; (2) cost-plus O&M contract; and (3) incentives/penalties O&M contract. Fixed-cost O&M contracts protect the project from O&M cost increases. Cost-plus contracts do not cap O&M costs while guaranteeing a profit margin for the operator and therefore do not create the right incentive structure to minimize costs. An O&M contract that contains both incentive bonus payments for operating to optimal design standards and operational performance as well as penalties for substandard operational performance offers a superior alignment of interests, which best protects the project lenders' exposure to O&M cost escalation risk and poor/substandard operational performance. One of the key lender protections against operational risk is the relative ease with which a project operator can be replaced—unlike other project contract parties, such as the project construction contractor or the project offtaker, there is generally a large pool of suitably qualified project operators with the required industry and technical experience to be able to step in and assume operational responsibilities.

OFFTAKE CONTRACTS/CONCESSION AGREEMENTS

As noted, there are essentially four basic forms of project revenue/offtake contract: (1) take or pay contracts (e.g., power projects) where both volume and price risk are assigned to the offtaker; (2) long-term sales or marketing contracts (e.g., mining as well as oil and gas projects) where volume risk is assigned to the offtaker but the project company (and therefore the lenders) assume commodity price risk; (3) availability-based contracts (e.g., gas pipelines, transmission lines) where "hell or high water" offtake payments are made by the offtaker as long as the project is available to perform the required service; and (4) concession contracts (e.g., toll roads, airports, ports) where the project assumes some level of revenue/traffic risk subject to limited government revenue support.

Irrespective of the project industry sector and associated offtake contract format, the offtake contract should include some basic provisions to protect the lenders. Specifically, the offtake contract term should ensure it matches the project life and the loan tenor plus a two-to-three-year residual "tail" to provide some slack should project performance fall short of the lenders base-case assumptions and a cash sweep/trap of the tail period is required to fully repay the outstanding loan. Offtake contracts should also ensure complete cost pass-through to the offtaker with respect to any fuel/feedstock supply obligations and that there is full contract alignment and harmonization for key provisions such as FM, change orders, and key project milestone dates such as final completion dates. One of the most heavily negotiated clauses in the offtake contract are the termination events and compensation for early termination. Offtake termination clauses should be very tightly drafted to limit the offtaker's ability to terminate; for example, offtaker termination should be limited until all cure remedies have been exhausted and only after extended natural FM periods (greater than 180 days) have been reached. The risk of termination for political FM events should be assigned to the offtaker (assuming it is a government or quasi-government entity) with a termination payment by the offtaker sized to at least cover the outstanding debt. While it is sometimes challenging to obtain a security assignment of the offtake contract (particularly if it is a concession contract), lenders should seek to ensure that the offtake agreement survives security enforcement and that the offtake contract can be transferred/assigned upon security enforcement.

SUPPLY CONTRACTS

Project feedstock/fuel supply contracts are critical project agreements as they represent the single largest component of operating costs for the project. Regardless of the nature of the supply arrangements, it is vitally important that the supply contract aligns and synchronizes with the revenue offtake contract, particularly in respect of FM provisions. The form of supply contract can take a number of forms including take or pay (important to ensure that project has full ability to pass through supply costs to offtaker and performance relief in the event the project is subject to dispatch risk by the offtaker) or tolling contracts (where there is no supply input cost and the project simply receives a processing fee). The form of supply commitment can also vary from flexible (minimum fixed supplies and balance variable, interruptible supply, etc.) to fixed subject to the specific needs of the project and the terms of the offtake contract. Security of supply and ensuring backup fuel/feedstock supplies on site is key to mitigate potential supply interruptions—it is typical for power projects to have 60-to-90-day backup fuel supply on the project site to mitigate short-term fuel supply interruptions. Termination events in the supply contract is another key issue, and supplier termination events should be narrowly defined and limited to material events such as failure to pay, abandonment, and insolvency.

PROJECT FINANCE LOAN DOCUMENTATION

The project finance loan documentation process is key to identifying and anticipating all project risks and allocating those risks to the parties best able to bear them. Loan documentation will be driven by the extent to which project risks have been allocated away to project counterparties or retained by the project company borrower; for example, if construction risks have been transferred to the construction contractor via a fixed price, date-certain EPC contract, then the need to include sponsor support guarantees for construction risk as part of the project loan documentation will be reduced. Before commencing negotiation of loan documentation, it is important for project lenders to assess and determine the fundamental technical, financial, economic, legal, political, and social and environmental viability of the project: Are management/sponsors experienced? Proven technology? Strong economic demand? Social and political support? Strong and reliable partners? and so forth. The lenders' due diligence process and outcomes is key to identifying any and all residual project risks that need to be closed off in the loan documentation process (for example, need for sponsor construction completion support, additional monitoring and reporting requirements for E&S risks, etc.). There are other avenues to address risk issues that are surfaced during the lender due diligence process if it cannot be achieved through the loan documents, including trying to go back and amend project contracts to allocate risk more effectively or adjusting the project financials (introduce higher DSCRs, cash sweeps/traps, re-leverage debt-to-equity ratio) to reflect the unresolved risks. Finally, while rare, it is not unheard of for lenders to make the ultimate decision to walk away from a project deal if there are insurmountable due diligence issues, unsustainable E&S issues, or untenable reputational risks.

There are several strategic approaches to negotiating and drafting project loan documentation. Lenders and project sponsors can either seek to negotiate a high-level short form financing term sheet with key commercial terms agreed and move quickly to full loan documentation or alternatively negotiate a more detailed and comprehensive long form term sheet and then convert this into the full-blown loan documentation. One of the abiding lessons from many years spent negotiating loan agreements is to first negotiate and agree the business deal and key finance terms between the lenders and the sponsors and only then bring in the lawyers to paper and document the deal—it will considerably reduce the length and complexity of the documentation process and as importantly, the legal bill to the project company!

The crafting of the project loan documentation, which sets forth the security and loan covenant package and defines the financial and operational decision-making capacity of the project company, needs to strike a balance between efficiently and effectively allocating risks away to project parties without triggering demands for higher risk-adjusted returns while at the same time not leaving the project company burdened with excessive residual project risks, which impair the SPV project company's financial sustainability. Lenders also need to be mindful of the law of unintended consequences—by placing excessively burdensome financial and operational decision-making restrictions on the project company, lenders could inadvertently impair the project's ability to optimally operate as efficiently as possible, and this is not in the lender's interest. As such, negotiating loan documentation is a balancing act and is as much art as science—the required skills can only be acquired through broad experience structuring and negotiating loan documentation.

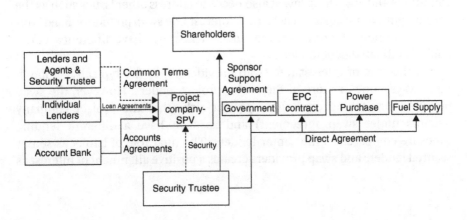

The key lynchpin project finance loan documents are as follows.

Common Terms Agreement

The common terms agreement (CTA) is an agreement between the project company and the lenders, which sets out the terms and conditions common to all financing instruments and constituent lenders in a multi-sourced project financing. The CTA is also sometimes referred to as the project coordination or co-financing agreement and serves to simplify and clarify a multi-source financing by ensuring that all lenders have a common understanding of the key definitions (disbursement procedures, reps and warranties, covenants, events of default, governing law, etc.) and critical events (voting rights for waivers and amendments, security enforcement and loan acceleration). The CTA will typically address disbursement procedures where some lenders such as ECAs are providing tied financing and as such, non–pro rata loan disbursements are required. The CTA also addresses loan repayments and mandatory prepayments, E&S safeguards, conditions precedent to financial close and initial and subsequent loan disbursements, reps and warranties, covenants and security, events of default, voting rights and security enforcement, and so forth.

The CTA allows the individual loan agreements for each lender to be much more limited in scope and only need address loan-specific terms and conditions such as the loan amount, tenor, and pricing with the bulk of the loan terms and conditions covered in the CTA. The operation and application of the CTA is usually overseen by the collateral agent or security trustee, which acts on behalf of the lenders. The collateral agent could be one of the project lenders or a non-lender third-party agent bank. While the CTA allows a disparate group of lenders to benefit from a single set of financing terms and conditions and governing law, it also needs to address other issues such as the voting rights and security treatment of interest rate swap providers, fixed- versus floating-rate interest loans, and lenders who might have different security and subordinated debt lenders.

In the case of interest rate swap providers, they are typically—though not always—one or more of the senior project lenders. However, the swap providers are taking contingent project risk (that the project company defaults under swap agreement) and as such have a different lending exposure compared to the senior lenders. The dual role of banks as senior secured lenders and swap providers creates a positive alignment of interest as it serves to protect swap providers' exposure and interests through the ability to represent their security interests and voting rights by virtue of also being senior lenders. In the event there is a swap default leading to a termination payment obligation from the project company to the swap providers, the termination payment will crystalize as a senior loan payment obligation of the project company ranking pari passu with the outstanding senior debt. The mechanics governing voting and security rights as between senior lenders and swap providers is normally addressed in the CTA. Similarly, if there is a tranche of mezzanine financing in the form of subordinated debt, senior lenders will require that the subordinated debt is "deep and dark" quasi-equity in that it cannot act on or call an event of default or take any loan acceleration or security enforcement that would negatively affect the senior lenders' preferred security position and rights. These rights and provisions as between senior lenders and subordinated debt providers would need to be clearly spelled out in the CTA.

Account Agreement and the "Cash Flow Waterfall"

The account agreement is a critical project agreement in project finance structuring. It is usually referred to as the cash flow waterfall and sets out the pre-agreed order of how project revenues and cash flows are to be applied/spent and reserved for in order to meet all project expenses, debt servicing, reserve requirements, and shareholder distributions. An account bank is typically appointed to administer and oversee the account agreement and ensure the terms of the agreement—in particular the application of the cash flow waterfall provisions—are applied correctly. The account bank is usually—though not always—one of the lending banks with an established agency department set up to manage the account bank functions. The chart below delineates a typical cash waterfall priority treatment of project revenues. The various required project reserve accounts (OMRA, DSRA, etc.) vary from project to project and can be pre-funded either as part of total project costs or built up from project cash flows. Project sponsors may also elect to pre-fund the required reserve accounts on a direct, recourse corporate basis by either providing a corporate guarantee or issuing an on-demand standby letter of credit. By providing a corporate guarantee or a standby letter of credit, the project IRR is improved as these are non-funded contingent obligations.

Project Finance Cash Flow Waterfall

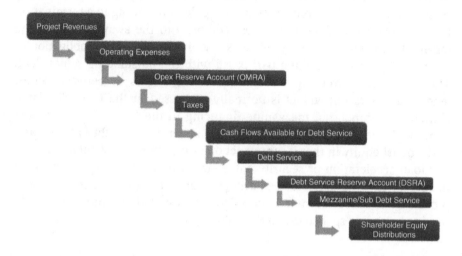

Shareholder equity distributions at the end of the cash flow waterfall are subject to certain preconditions such as there being no event of default and meeting a minimum DSCR test (dividend distribution test). The rationale for the dividend distribution test is to ensure the project is meeting minimum operational performance and cash flow generation before any cash flows are released to the equity investors while also preserving cash within the project should project cash flows become stressed. For example, a power project might set a dividend distribution test at 1.25x. This ensures that any deterioration in the operational and financial performance such that, say, the actual DSCR declines to 1.20x would prohibit dividend distributions to shareholders and trap this cash in the project. Should this blip in financial performance be temporary and the actual DSCR for the next test period returns to 1.30x, then the accumulated, trapped dividend distributions would be released as the 1.25x dividend distribution test has now been met. However, if this is in fact a systemic decline in project cash flows and the dividend distribution test fails to be met a second or third time, then the cash remains trapped and will be either used to prepay debt or to remedy the performance shortfall should there be a technical solution. The market standard in most project finance deals is that two consecutive periods of failing to meet the dividend distribution test triggers a mandatory debt prepayment (usually in inverse order of debt maturity) from the funds trapped in the distribution account. As you might imagine, this is a contentious and heavily negotiated loan documentation issue between lenders and sponsors.

The cash flow waterfall is typically run every 6 months, when debt service is paid and the DSCR test is applied. One of the other issues that surfaces is the basis for the DSCR test—forward-looking next 6 months, historic last 6 months, or rolling average 6 months. Most project deals use historic last 6 months as the basis for the DSCR test as the assumptions for forward testing are difficult to define and agree with project sponsors and a forward DSCR test is generally less informative/accurate compared to historic/actual project financial performance.

Direct Agreements

Direct agreements are typically tri-partite financing agreements executed between the lenders, the project company, and the relevant project contract counterparty. The purpose of the direct agreement is to acknowledge project lenders' security rights and provide certain consent, remedy, and cure rights to lenders with respect to the project contract. Direct agreements are usually executed with respect to the key project contracts such as the EPC contract, the offtake or concession contract, and the O&M contract. The purpose is to address and acknowledge the following project lender consents and rights:

- Consent for project company to assign contract by way of security to the lenders;
- Consent to assign the contract to third parties in the event of default by the project company;
- Additional grace and cure periods for lenders to remedy defaults before terminating the contract;
- Inclusion of clarification and additional lender negotiated points; and
- Any lender requirements of the offtaker such as irrevocable requirement for offtaker to direct project revenues into a lender-approved bank account, no amendments or waivers to contract without lender approvals, notification requirements to lenders for contract defaults as well as lender step-in rights to cure defaults, etc.

Covenants and Security Package

Given that project finance involves lending to a thinly capitalized, highly leveraged borrower with (typically) construction risk and no cash flows, project finance lenders will require a comprehensive covenant and security package. Project finance lender security covers four main layers of protection: (1) a mortgage interest and assignment pledge over all physical project assets, contracts, and insurance policies; (2) assignment of project company shares; (3) control over all project revenues and cash flows via the account agreement and consent; and (4) step-in rights to remedy and cure potential defaults and ability to replace project counterparties and assign contracts to third parties. Project security is a defensive protection for lenders in that lenders do not want to end up owning the project and assuming the associated risks and liabilities; rather, it provides lenders with "nuisance value" and important protections. Project finance is a form of cash flow financing as opposed to asset financing, and the critical lifeline for project lenders is the cash flows that derive from the underlying project contracts, therefore preserving the critical project contracts (particularly the revenues offtake contract) is key. The critical protections that project security provides to lenders are as follows:

- Gives lenders a "stick" or a "seat at the table" in the event there is a major issue with the project that triggers a default and potential security enforcement;
- Protects project lenders from any third-party claims or liens against the project assets and contracts and ensures project lender claims will always rank senior to other creditors;
- Ensures project assets are not sold or divested without prior lender approvals; and
- Encourages a basis for alignment of interests across all project stakeholders to be able to negotiate equitable resolutions of major issues that could arise.

The covenants included in the project financing agreements form part of the lenders' security package in that they give lenders veto control over the project cash flow waterfall and certain actions that the project company can undertake. They also help to ensure the project company does not deviate from its core activities, which are owning and operating the underlying infrastructure project asset. Key market standard financial covenants and undertakings include:

- Comply with project documents and not amend or waive without lender approval;
- Limitations on additional debt and asset sales;

- Maintenance of insurances, reporting requirements, annual budget review/approval;
- Maintenance of a debt service reserve account;
- Minimum and average debt service coverage ratio;
- Dividend restrictions;
- Negative pledge; and
- Cash trap/sweep (if applicable).

KEY LENDER PROTECTION MECHANISMS AND STRATEGIES FOR NEGOTIATING FINANCE AGREEMENTS

The project loan agreements contain representations and warranties, covenants, and events of default that provide lenders with the ability to control matters should something go wrong with the project and an event of default is triggered. The challenge with crafting the right balance of effective control over the project company for lenders—while also not unnecessarily hamstringing the project company from operating optimally and potentially triggering an unintended technical default—is more art than science and based on the experience of project finance parties (lenders, legal counsel, sponsors) negotiating the deal. The key objective when negotiating and drafting the various warranties, covenants, and events of default is to achieve the optimum balance of these lender protections/controls while also providing adequate flexibility and leeway to the project company to operate the project to optimize operational and financial performance.

As noted, one of the key lender protections is control over the project revenues and cash flows. This is achieved by requiring the project company to open segregated bank accounts pledged to the project lenders and overseen and controlled by the designated collateral agent or account bank. These cash flow control protections are enshrined in the account agreement, which predetermines the priority order of application of project revenues administered by the account bank. The account bank will strictly apply project revenues in compliance with the account agreement. As you might expect, the payment of operating expenses ranks very high in the cash flow waterfall given it is critical to maintain operations under all circumstances to ensure continued generation of cash flows and to avoid the risk that the offtaker could terminate the revenue offtake contract. Similarly, dividend distributions rank very low in the order of payment priority in the cash flow waterfall, typically at the end of the waterfall after all other payment obligations (operation expenses, debt service, refilling reserve accounts, etc.) have been satisfied. There is sometimes some debate as to the order of payment priority across different classes of lender creditors; however, it is typically that interest is paid before principal repayments and payment is pro rata for all pari passu senior secured lenders. Any mezzanine-level subordinated debt is structurally subordinated to senior debt and sits between senior debt and shareholder dividend distributions in the cash flow waterfall.

The legal jurisdiction governing the project loan agreements is typically either New York or UK law. There are several reasons for this, primarily that the established legal systems in these jurisdictions are proven in dealing with complex project finance deals. This provides comfort to project lenders concerning precedent treatment and legal rulings that security can be perfected and enforced as designed and intended. Security documents' legal jurisdiction on the other hand is normally governed by the location of the project and the physical and other assets being pledged to lenders. Therefore, it is important to use local legal counsel in the project country location to ensure that lenders have effective onshore and offshore security over the project assets.

Case Study: Samba Drillship Oil and Gas Project, Brazil

The Samba case study provides a good example of how project lender security rights work in practice when tested by a project loan default. It also reveals the challenges and issues faced by lenders in exercising and enforcing security rights over project company shares and assets.

Project Overview and Background

Samba is an $852 million deep-water drillship project in Brazil sponsored by Samba Drilling SA ("main sponsor") and Mitsubishi Corporation ("Mitsubishi"). The project was funded with 80% project finance debt ($689 million) and reached financial close in December 2012. The proceeds from the financing were used to construct a deep-water drillship on a lump-sum turnkey basis at Samsung Heavy Industries Co., Ltd.'s Goeje Shipyard in Korea. Upon completion, the drillship was to be chartered to Petroleo Brasileiro S.A. ("Petrobras") under a charter contract and a related service contract for an initial term of 10 years with an option to renew for another 10 years. Samsung is a world-class special vessel contractor with a strong market reputation of on-time and on-budget delivery. Samsung also provided a full refund guarantee from The Export-Import Bank of Korea ("KEXIM") in relation to the construction contract. Petrobras (rated BBB/Baa1 at the time) is Brazil's national oil company and one of the largest publicly traded oil companies in the world with large offshore reserves and new deep-water oil discoveries, which required a large number of drillships and semi submersibles for exploration and development drilling.

Petrobras is considered one of the top twenty largest oil and gas companies in the world, with a current market capitalization of over $100 billion.

Samba Drillship – Project Overview

The drillship was constructed under a lump-sum turnkey contract by Samsung in South Korea. Upon completion and acceptance by Petrobras, the drillship was chartered to Petrobras and operated by Samba Engenharia under two 10-year contracts, respectively. The deployment of the drillship is planned to expand the drilling areas in the deep water of the offshore Campos Basin in water depths up to 3,000 meters where Petrobras lacks this deep-water drilling capability among the units in its chartered and owned fleet. Under the charter contract and service contract, Petrobras will pay Samba a total day rate of $415,000. Petrobras will pay a bonus of up to 10% if drillship availability rate is 93–98%.

(continued)

(continued)

Over the last 10 years, Petrobras has concentrated development investments in the deep-water fields located in the offshore Campos Basin where
over 80% of its total domestic proved reserves are located. As detailed in
its business plan for 2008–2012, Petrobras planned to spend over 58% of
its total planned investments in the E&P activities ($112.4 billion in total),
84% of which will be in Brazil. This level of investments is needed by Petrobras to support active development programs in existing fields as well as
in the discovery and recovery of new reserve finds. Petrobras' business
plan demonstrated a strong future demand for offshore exploration and
production equipment.

Samba Project Finance Risk Mitigation

Below are the key structural risks evaluated with respect to the Samba
project along with risk mitigation factors:

- ***Construction Risk***—Mitigated as follows:
  - Lump-sum EPC contract—the drillship will be built by Sam-
    sung Heavy Industries Co., Ltd., on a lump-sum turnkey basis.
    Samsung is a key member of the Samsung Group, which is the
    largest business conglomerate in Korea, and has a good mar-
    ket reputation and outstanding track record of delivering sim-
    ilar drillships on budget and schedule. Since 2005, Samsung
    has constructed about 80% of deep-water drilling ships world-
    wide, which contributes to its well-respected market and tech-
    nology position among the top three leading yards worldwide
    in this segment;
  - Refund Guarantee—completion risk mitigated by a refund
    guarantee issued by KEXIM. In the event that Samsung fails
    to deliver the drillship by the pre-agreed delivery date, the
    buyer can call on the refund guarantee, which is structured
    to cover the total loan outstanding during the construction
    period;
  - Cost contingencies—equal to 5% of the EPC price built into
    the overall project cost, which will be available to cover any
    cost overruns;
  - Acceptance risk mitigated—the drillship will be built based
    on Petrobras' technical specifications in the RFP (request for

proposal) and will be fully tested according to a simulated 72-hour acceptance test in South Korea before Samba's acceptance; and

- Proven technology—the drillship is based on Samsung/ Reading and Bates Saipem 10000 design, of which more than 20 drillships have already been built or/and are on order. The Saipem 10000 design is well known to Samsung. The design is also well known and acceptable to Petrobras.

- *Revenue Risk*—Mitigated as follows:
  - 10-year (with 10-year renewal option) firm take or pay charter contract with Petrobras;
  - Fixed USD charter payments sufficient to cover debt service based on drillship availability with no oil and gas commodity price risk or reserve/production risk;
  - Petrobras 30-year track record of never defaulting on a charter payment or terminating a charter contract;
  - Charter payments are effectively operating expenses for Petrobras, so structurally senior in payment priority to Petrobras' senior debt payment obligations;
  - Cost competitive day-rate well below international market day-rates for comparable drillship vessels; and
  - Sustainable, long-term demand for deep-water drilling rigs to explore and develop offshore oil discoveries in Brazil's Campos Basin and Pre-Salt (largest Western Hemisphere oil discovery in the past 30-years) areas.

- *Operator Risk*—Mitigated as follows:
  - Samba is an experienced and successful offshore operator. For about 15 years, they have operated a drillship with dynamic positioning system that uses much of the same technology that will be applied to the platforms for about 15 years; and
  - Samba has consistently scored as one of the top independent offshore operators for Petrobras as measured by downtime and safety.

- *Political Risk*—Mitigated as follows:
  - Brazil's and Petrobras's investment grade sovereign credit rating;

(continued)

(*continued*)

- Brazil and Petrobras's 30-year unblemished payment history of never defaulting on—or rescheduling/restructuring—charter payment obligations; and
- Preferential treatment of charter payments as trade-related payments that have priority access to USD remittances by the Central Bank of Brazil, which mitigates currency convertibility and transfer risk.

Project Outcomes

Financial close was achieved in December 2012 with the drillship construction completed on schedule and on budget in 2013. The $692 million financing was provided by a consortium of commercial banks along with non-bank financial institutions and KEXIM. KEXIM provided financing based on the role of Samsung as the EPC contractor. The drillship commenced commercial operation in 2013, drilling wells in deep-water blocks offshore Brazil for Petrobras.

The drillship and the project financing contractual framework operated and functioned successfully until early 2014 when a confluence of black swan events served to cause unprecedented stress testing to the project's financial sustainability and the integrity of the project contracts and the lenders' security package. Specifically, the following developments occurred:

- International oil prices declined dramatically in April 2014 from $110 per barrel to $50 per barrel, precipitating a decline in day rates for deep-water drilling rigs from approximately $600,000 in Spring 2014 to about $400,000 in 2015 with drilling rig market utilization rates declining from close to 100% capacity utilization in 2014 to 80% by early 2015. Samba's day rate of $421,000 remained competitive relative to international market rates even after the market decline.
- Simultaneously, in April 2014 one of the largest corruption scandals in Latin America's history involving Petrobras, major Brazilian engineering and construction companies, and Brazilian politicians broke. The corruption and bribery scandal was dubbed "Lava Jato," which means car wash in Portuguese, as the corruption scheme was unearthed following a money laundering investigation where proceeds of the scheme were

being laundered through Brazilian car wash facilities. The Lava Jato scheme involved collusion between Petrobras officials and Brazilian construction companies to rig contract awards to those companies who in turn inflated the contract price by 3–5%, which served as the kick-back payment to the Petrobras officials involved with the scheme. The scheme ensnared most—if not all—major Brazilian construction companies including one of the largest (Odebrecht) and involved embezzlement of Petrobras funds to the tune of over $2.5 billion and spanned 11 countries in Latin America. The high-profile casualties of this corruption scandal included Marcel Odebrecht, CEO of the largest Brazilian construction company, Odebrecht, who was sentenced to 19 years in prison for paying $30 million in bribes to Petrobras officials along with former Brazilian president Lula.

The impact of these two simultaneous commodity market and political crisis events had a significantly detrimental impact on Petrobras's financial condition. Petrobras delayed releasing its 2014 annual results and in April 2015 released audited financial statements showing $2.1 billion in bribes and a write down of $17 billion due to overvalued assets. Due to the high debt burden that Petrobras had taken on to develop offshore oil reserves, the company was forced into an emergency capital expenditure reduction and asset sale program of almost $14 billion to conserve cash and reduce debt.

Samba had two main lines of business, being offshore oil and gas drilling along with a separate engineering and construction business. The engineering business of Samba was caught up in the Lava Jato scandal and in an effort to save the business and stave off bankruptcy, the owners tried to cross-subsidize the business with cash flows from the drilling business unbeknownst to the project lenders. The siphoning of project cash flows from Samba and the company's other rigs, along with the escalating financial difficulties of the engineering business and over $2 billion in corporate debt, led Samba to cut back operation and maintenance expenditure for its rigs, including Samba. In April 2015 Samba, without either notice to—or approval from—the lenders, halted operations on all its operating rigs, including Samba, amid a liquidity and cash flow crisis. Ten days later Samba filed for bankruptcy.

(continued)

(continued)

Petrobras, focused on capex reduction opportunities, used the unilateral cessation of rig operations as an opportunity to terminate the charter contracts for all rigs, including Samba. The project lenders sought to exercise their remedy rights afforded under the direct agreement with Petrobras by replacing Samba as the project operator and in doing so cure the termination event and preserve the critical charter contracts. Usually the security agreements would function normally, and lenders would be given the opportunity to cure the default. However, these were unprecedented times for Brazil and Petrobras, and there was no willingness or capacity on the part of Petrobras to honor the lenders' security rights and engage with the lenders or seek a solution that would reverse the termination notice and preserve the charter contract.

Having exhausted all options and faced with the termination of the charter contract with little prospect of re-contracting the drillship in Brazil, the lenders sought to take possession of the drillship by enforcing their assigned security interests in the shares and mortgage over the project company and the project assets. This was a complicated legal and operational challenge as the project sponsors sought to block lenders in the Brazilian courts as the drillship was physically sitting in Brazilian waters about 300 km offshore. The sanctity of the security documents was upheld by the Brazilian courts, and lenders successfully took legal possession of the drillship asset. The next step was to secure operational control and take the drillship out of Brazilian waters so that it could be redeployed in another key deep-water drilling location—the "golden triangle" of Gulf of Mexico or Offshore Africa. The lenders and their representatives secured the service of a third-party rig asset manager/operator who helicoptered in a new crew onto the rig, paid and flew to shore the Brazilian crew, and then spirited the drillship out of Brazilian waters to a port in the Caribbean where it could be laid up and inspected while the lenders determined their next course of action. It was very much drama on the high seas more akin to a Jason Bourne plot than mundane project financing!

The offshore drilling market continued its decline through the remainder of 2015 and into 2016 with day rates plummeting to below $300,000 and the industry utilization rates below 60% as integrated oil and gas majors cut back capital spending due to low oil prices and speculative rigs constructed without contracts in the peak 2012–2014 period were delivered to owners—further exacerbating the oversupply situation. Project lenders were unsuccessful in re-contracting Samba in the midst of this market collapse. Due to the significant costs associated with maintaining and laying up the drillship, the lenders elected to seek a buyer for the unit via a public auction. In April 2016, the Samba drillship was sold for $65 million to another offshore driller. The fire sale price for a relatively new, state-of-the-art deep-water rig represented barely 10% of the original construction cost just 3 years earlier. By this point most lenders had either written off their loan exposures or sold their loans for cents on the dollar.

Key Takeaways and Lessons Learned

In project financing we often learn more from deals that fail versus those that are successful. This was certainly the case with the Samba project. Samba, along with a large number of other Brazilian rig financings, was undone by unforeseen black swan events outside and beyond the lenders' control. Ultimately, Brazilian political risk conspired with weak oil commodity markets to precipitate an unprecedented collapse in the offshore drilling market—in 2012 Brazil and Petrobras accounted for well over 60% of the deep-water rig market, contracting 80 deep-water drillships and semi-submersibles; by 2017 that number had dropped by almost two-thirds to 30 rigs under contract by Petrobras.

The key takeaways and lessons learned from the Samba case study are as follows:

- The project lenders' security rights and protections worked. Despite legal challenges, lenders were able to step in and exercise and enforce their security rights and ultimately secure ownership and possession of the drillship;
- The importance to conduct detailed due diligence on your project sponsor—even on unrelated business activities. The lenders felt they had created a financial firewall between Samba's corporate financials and the project company by requiring all project equity be subscribed upfront with no further financial reliance (such as guarantees) other than operational risk on Samba. The contagion effect of the failing engineering and construction business ultimately precipitated a cash flow problem that negatively affected the operational activities of Samba;

(continued)

(*continued*)

- Lenders like drillship lending given the mobile asset nature of these deals, with the ability and optionality to be redeployed to other more favorable offshore markets. It is a highly cyclical industry, and market downturns tend to occur on a global basis as opposed to regional downturns.

CHAPTER 4

Risks and Challenges of Project Financing in Emerging Markets

Project finance has proved to be effective when applied to countries with heightened political risks, underdeveloped legal and regulatory systems, and weak or nascent creditor rights. The successful execution of project financing transactions poses very specific and unique challenges in emerging markets. Political and cross-border risks present the biggest volatility factors and unpredictable risks, which can produce adverse outcomes for investors.

The bespoke nature of project finance in emerging markets and the required higher intensity level of customized risk mitigation to structure out political and cross-border risks makes it difficult to achieve the required standardization, scalability, and velocity of transactional volume to meet institutional investor appetite for infrastructure project finance assets. The sub-investment grade ratings of most emerging markets also make it difficult to access deeper and more liquid institutional investor pools of capital such as the capital markets.

TRACK RECORD OF PROJECT FINANCE IN EMERGING MARKETS—THE ASIAN IPP EXPERIENCE

The application of project financing techniques to infrastructure investments in emerging markets gained traction in the early to mid-1990s. Major infrastructure initiatives in Asia such as Pakistan's private power IPP program, which attracted over 25 private sector projects representing almost 5,000 MWs of installed capacity and $5 billion in private investment and Indonesia's and the Philippines' IPP programs, which achieved similar investment outcomes, were instrumental in elevating the focus of project finance lending capital toward emerging markets. Private investment in power generation during this period made a significant and sustainable contribution to developing countries' infrastructure needs and fundamentally transformed the ownership and operational control of the power generation sector in nearly all emerging markets. According to the World Bank, private investor participation in the power sector between 1990 and 1997 amounted to $131 billion of private power contracts in emerging markets—a large amount of this investment capital was financed via project financing from commercial banks, MDBs (multilateral development banks), BDBs (bilateral development banks), and ECAs[1] (export credit agencies). The height of the IPP boom occurred between 1992 and 1996, when the firm power contract market for large greenfield IPPs consisted of 137 projects constituting 67 GWs of generation capacity worth $65 billion. While the IPP impact was global in nature, Asia dominated the market with 103 contracts worth $54 billion—Latin America was a distant second with 28 contracts representing $6.6 billion of investment. Seven countries in Asia dominated the IPP market, namely, China, Indonesia, Philippines, India, Pakistan, Malaysia, and Thailand while in Latin America the main markets were the more market-friendly countries of Argentina, Columbia, and Chile. While Asian IPPs largely sold power generation under long-term, take or pay offtake contracts to vertically integrated government-owned utilities, the IPP market in Latin America was based on power sales to private sector offtakers and disaggregated public utilities at the prevailing market power pool price.

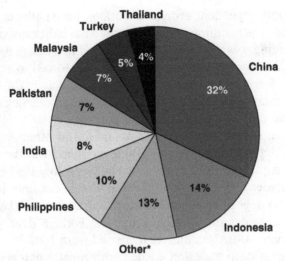

Source: Based on World Bank, Energy, Mining, and Telecommunications Department, Knowledge, Management database.

IPPs mobilized $55 billon of private funds, of which project finance represented approximately 62%.[2]

CURRENCY MISMATCH—LESSONS LEARNED FROM THE ASIAN CURRENCY CRISIS

The Asian currency crisis was a major financial crisis that affected all major economies across East Asia and Southeast Asia between 1997 and 1998. The financial crisis began in July 1997 in Thailand when the government was forced to drop its US dollar-Thai baht currency peg and allow the Thai baht currency to float due to declining foreign currency reserves and an inability to defend the local currency. At the time, the major Asian economies—known as the Asian Tigers—had fixed or pegged their currencies to the US dollar. The origins of the Asian currency crisis had its basis in short-term capital or "hot money," which flowed into Asian countries to take advantage of the interest rate arbitrage play between high domestic interest rates and low US funding rates. Local companies in Thailand and other Asian countries also assumed significant foreign currency debt due to more favorable offshore interest rates, which in turn created an asset bubble. Following concerns about the export dependent economic outlook for Thailand, capital flight quickly ensued. The resulting pressure on the Thai baht caused the currency to depreciate rapidly as the central bank engaged in a losing battle to defend the currency, and the government was ultimately forced to abandon its US dollar peg as foreign currency reserves were depleted. Currency traders who took speculative positions against the Thai baht also exacerbated and accelerated the currency's collapse. The currency crisis quickly spread to South Korea, Indonesia, Malaysia, Philippines, and other Asian countries with currency depreciations averaging 40%. Indonesia was the hardest hit as the Indonesia rupiah declined by over 80% between July 1997 and July 1998. As local companies had most of their debt in foreign currency loans, the cost of servicing that debt in local currency terms increased markedly, resulting in significant debt defaults and bankruptcies. Foreign debt-to-GDP levels in the four largest ASEAN countries increased from 100% to 180% between 1993 and 1998. A deep recession ensued with most Asian economies only recovering in 2000–2001.

The currency collapse caused domestic retail power prices to increase dramatically due to the high foreign exchange content (fuel cost, offshore financing) of IPPs. State-owned utilities in Asia struggled to pass through the bulk power tariff increases arising from the currency collapse to customers—particularly to politically sensitive residential and agricultural customers—and instead engaged in cross-subsidization by increasing power rates for industrial and commercial customers. The response from the industrial and commercial users—who had large electricity requirements for cost effective and stable power generation—was to seek to develop their own inside-the-fence captive power and thus avoid grid supply and further shrink utilities' revenue base.

One of the critical questions ex ante is whether IPPs and the underlying project finance deals were successful in allocating project risks to the private sector. Most Asian IPP projects were structured based on full pass-through of fuel costs, take or pay offtake contracts with firm capacity payments regardless of power dispatch sufficient to cover the cost of debt and equity capital, as well as protection for currency changes via indexation between the USD and local currency. IPPs in many cases were also protected against political risks by government counter-guarantees against payment default by the public utility offtakers, thereby effectively creating massive public sector contingent debt liabilities, which arguably negated the original intention to finance these projects with private capital. The World Bank in particular was highly critical of these government guarantee arrangements as they impaired public sector borrowing capacity for important poverty reduction social programs such as housing, healthcare, and education. The combination of foreign currency external debt and USD-denominated fuel costs characteristic of IPPs at the time exposed countries to significant foreign exchange risks. Other than China, Malaysia, and Thailand, most countries had undeveloped local capital markets to source local currency financing and so were highly dependent on offshore foreign currency financing. Asian IPPs were also heavily dependent on imported fossil fuel supply, further compounding the foreign currency risk exposure. Some of this was self-inflicted, as in the case of Pakistan, which had abundant indigenous resources of natural gas and hydro resources but chose to base its IPP program on imported fuel oil, which represented 74% of all IPPs developed in Pakistan.

IPPs did serve to deliver meaningful benefits to Asian countries. Specifically, IPPs introduced new generation technologies and efficiencies, particularly around gas turbines and clean coal generation technologies. IPPs also heralded critical electricity regulatory reform and greater price transparency.

HOW THE ASIAN CURRENCY CRISIS TRANSFORMED THE APPROACH TO PROJECT FINANCE

The 1997–1998 Asian currency crisis had a profound and long-lasting effect on how IPPs are structured and negotiated and fundamentally transformed the approach to project financing these and other infrastructure projects. The fallout and effect from the currency crisis was not uniform across four of the largest and most affected IPP countries—Thailand, Indonesia, Malaysia, and the Philippines.[3] The broad effects can be grouped as follows:

- Increased cost of power
- Incidences of contract default and power tariff renegotiation
- Impact on private power investments

The impact of a major currency devaluation, such as occurred during the Asian currency crisis, resulted in a significant increase in the cost of goods and services in local currency terms, particularly electric power costs. The relative increase in cost of power varied significantly across the four countries and was a function of the dimensions of the crisis, the source of fuel supply, onshore versus offshore financing, currency denomination of power tariffs, and the relationship between wholesale power tariffs and consumer retail tariffs. Indonesia and the Philippines were most severely affected by the increased cost of power—Indonesia, for example, would have required a 70% increase in retail power tariffs to offset the effect of the 80% currency devaluation. This was due mainly to the fact that wholesale IPP power tariffs in Indonesia and the Philippines were either denominated in hard currency or had full indexation to hard currency while power tariffs in Malaysia and Thailand were expressed or denominated in local currency equivalent. The other major driver is the degree of onshore versus offshore financing. Both Malaysia and Thailand had fairly well-developed local capital markets and could raise long-term local currency financing for project financing while Indonesia and the Philippines were solely reliant on foreign currency financing due to a lack of a local capital market. The Philippines and Thailand were disproportionally affected by fuel costs, which were mostly based on imported fuel subject to currency adjustment and full cost pass-through under the terms of the offtake contracts with IPPs. These factors helped to mute the currency devaluation effect on the cost of power in Malaysia and Thailand while exacerbating it in Indonesia and the Philippines.

TABLE 1   CRISIS-RELATED FACTORS AFFECTING THE IMPACT OF IPP COSTS ON RETAIL TARIFFS

Country	Dimensions of crisis	Fuel supply	Denomination of payments	Source of financing	Project vintage	Wholesale tariffs	Overall impact
Indonesia	●	○	●	●	●	●	●
Malaysia	◐	○	○	○	○	○	○
Philippines	◐	●	●	●	◐	◐	◐/●
Thailand	●	●	○	◐	◐	○	◐/○

○ Little Impact   ◐ Some Impact   ● Severe Impact

The severe financial effect on public sector utilities from the financial crisis led to efforts to renegotiate wholesale power tariffs with IPPs. This was most pronounced in Indonesia, where the state-owned utility PLN was negatively affected by the 80% devaluation of the Indonesian rupiah. PLN initially tried to unilaterally set an FX rate of 2,450 as the basis (the rupiah FX rate was trading at 8,450 at the time) for negotiating wholesale tariffs before reversing course.[4] The fact that most IPPs in Indonesia and the Philippines were awarded without competitive bidding exposed private power investments in those countries to charges of corruption and lack of transparency and ultimately forced IPPs to renegotiate the original power tariffs. On the other hand, private power contracts in Malaysia and Thailand were subject to international competitive bidding and thus achieved lower initial wholesale power tariffs and thus resulted in fewer defaults and tariff renegotiations.

The Asian currency crisis and the subsequent recession resulted in falling economic growth and reduced demand for electricity. This created a large imbalance in power supply and demand and resulted in many IPP projects being delayed, postponed, or canceled. The economic slowdown is estimated to have reduced regional power needs from over 16 GW to about 7 GW and would take up to 5 years for most countries to absorb the excess power supply. While it is difficult for power policies to anticipate a financial crisis of the scale of the Asian currency crisis, there were some fundamental lessons learned, which would reshape the methodology and underpinnings of project finance as follows:

- Focus on creating natural currency hedges by matching currency mixes across project costs, funding sources, and offtake revenues, seeking to source local currency funding and developing local capital markets
- Too much too soon—Recognition that too much generating capacity was brought online too quickly creating financial stress on state-owned utilities subject to take or pay offtake contract terms, which only served to increase power generation reserve margins. For example, in Pakistan the state-owned utility WAPDA's (Water and Power Development Authority) share of power from IPPs increased from 20% in 1997 to over 45% in 2000 with IPPs representing 50% of WAPDA's operating costs.[5]
- Prioritize regulatory reform—Many of the state-owned utility offtakers were financially weak, were reliant on government subsidies for financial sustainability, and their true costs did not reflect the fully loaded avoided cost of power generation. This was due in part to a systemic culture of high technical (transmission and distribution line losses) and non-technical losses (electricity theft), weak bill collection/unpaid arrears, and electricity treated as political patronage in countries such as India. Non-technical losses were as high as 30% in many countries. The need to reform the electricity sector by reducing government subsidies and requiring vertically integrated utilities to de-bundle generation, transmission, and distribution activities to drive competition and improve financial sustainability was recognized as a necessary and required prerequisite before IPP

programs could be successful. The World Bank was a strong advocate and proponent of this required electricity sector reform.

- Willingness versus ability to pay—One of the enduring lessons from the Asian currency crisis for project finance lenders is the need to ensure commercial viability versus contractual viability. If the effective price of power charged by IPPs is materially higher than the utility's retail power tariffs, then the contractual framework is not sustainable, and it is a highly likely inevitability that the power price in the offtake agreement will need to be renegotiated—particularly when the state-owned utility's financial condition is precarious to begin with.

- Transparent competitive bidding—Most IPP projects in Asia in the 1990s were awarded on a negotiated basis, which subsequently raised concerns about political influence and accusations of corruption by successive governments. For example, rather than an open, competitive bidding process, Pakistan awarded IPP contracts based on projects meeting a levelized power tariff ceiling (6.1 cents/kWh under the 1994 Private Power Policy). This approach also failed to incentivize developers to reduce costs. In 1998 the government of Pakistan issued termination notices to about two-thirds of the IPP projects under development and construction alleging corruption under the guise of delaying the commissioning of IPPs and seeking to pressure IPPs to renegotiate unsustainable USD-denominated power tariffs affected by a 45% depreciation of the Pakistan rupee and WAPDA's worsening financial condition and liquidity. The need to ensure open and transparent competitive bidding processes for IPPs was one of the enduring lessons from the Asian IPP experiment.

ROLE OF MULTILATERAL, BILATERAL DEVELOPMENT BANKS, AND EXPORT CREDIT AGENCIES

The participation of MDBs, BDBs, and ECAs in project finance deals serves to mitigate political risk and adverse sovereign actions that can negatively affect project deals. Political risk mitigation can either be direct and explicit, as with PRI policies issued by ECAs and other PRI providers such as the Multilateral Insurance Guarantee Agency (MIGA) and private sector insurers, or implicit, as with joint co-financing from MDBs such as the IFC, ADB, and the IDB Invest or BDBs such as DEG of Germany, FMO of Holland, or Proparco of France.

ECA PRI policies typically cover the three pillars of political risk: currency convertibility and transfer; nationalization/expropriation; and war, riots, and civil unrest. ECAs typically will provide PRI cover up to the value of goods and services being exported from their country of origin in connection with the project. Some ECAs can provide either PRI guarantees or direct loans to the project. For example, US Exim Bank can either issue PRI policies or provide direct loans at the discretion of the project sponsors. ECAs are required to follow the OECD consensus guidelines for export credits, which dictate financing terms such as maximum loan tenors, loan amortization terms, and minimum premiums and interest rates. PRI premiums can either be paid upfront as a lump sum as part of project costs or paid annually from project cash flows. ECAs provide fixed rate financing based on the prevailing commercial interest reference rates, or CIRR (https://www.oecd.org/trade/topics/export-credits/arrangement-and-sector-understandings/financing-terms-and-conditions/). ECAs will normally require risk sharing with commercial banks when providing PRI coverage; typically, they will cover up to 85–90% of the loan amount being funded by the commercial banks with the banks assuming clean political risk exposure on the remaining 10–15% "top-up" financing. ECAs can also consider providing comprehensive cover (political and commercial or project risk cover) if so requested and required to catalyze commercial bank lending where country risks are so high that commercial banks would not otherwise participate in the deal. For example, an ECA might provide 85% PRI cover and 60% commercial risk cover with banks assuming 15% residual political risk and 40% commercial risk.

MDBs indirectly provide PRI cover to commercial banks by co-financing alongside the banks. Commercial banks view the "halo effect" of the MDB lending to the project as tantamount to political risk protection by virtue of the MDB's preferred creditor status—MDB lending is typically excluded from any sovereign debt restructuring/rescheduling, they have priority access to foreign exchange, and are usually exempted from capital controls by central banks. MDBs—as in the case of the IFC as a member of the World bank group—are usually a major source of bilateral sovereign lending and as such have considerable access and negotiating leverage with the host government to be able to address and intercede on any sovereign or political risk issues affecting the project. In addition, there are cross-default provisions such that an IFC project loan default could trigger a cross-default to all other World Bank loans—most high-risk emerging markets countries are heavily reliant on World Bank lending and as such are highly incentivized to minimize the risk of such a cross-default scenario. The same logic applies to IDB Invest in Central and Latin America and the ADB in Asia where IDB Invest and the ADB are the main sovereign creditor in their respective regions. MDBs—and to a lesser extent BDBs—view themselves as "lenders of last resort" and as such seek to crowd in and not crowd out private sector lending by commercial banks.

One common form of loan structure that MDBs such as the IFC and IDB Invest use to mobilize private sector bank financing is the A:B Loan Program. Under this program, the IFC or IDB Invest acts as the lender of record for both an A loan and a B loan to the project company. Commercial banks then risk participation in the B loan via a participation agreement with the IFC/IDB Invest while the A loan exposure remains with the IFC/IDB Invest. So IFC/IDB Invest effectively fronts the entire A and B loans, and as far as the project company and the host government is concerned, the IFC/IDB Invest is considered as lending the entire loan amount (A and B loans combined). Commercial banks benefit from the "umbrella" effect of the IFC/IDB Invest preferred creditor status and the risk mitigation derived from the fact that the project company would have to default on the IFC/IDB Invest loan in order to default on the commercial banks. One of the challenges with the A:B loan program is that commercial banks have to assign most voting rights (the IFC and IDB Invest will agree to certain consent rights; however, in order to preserve the sanctity of the IFC/IDB Invest lender of record status, they require banks to have limited explicit voting rights), although the IFC/IDB Invest will agree to consult with the commercial banks and provide timely information and notification as issues arise and decisions are required to be made.

IFC A:B Loan Structure

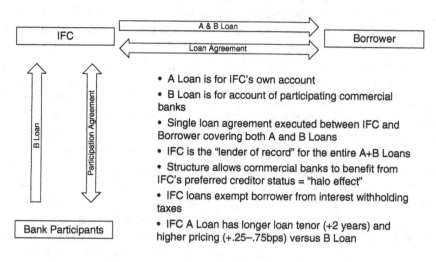

- A Loan is for IFC's own account
- B Loan is for account of participating commercial banks
- Single loan agreement executed between IFC and Borrower covering both A and B Loans
- IFC is the "lender of record" for the entire A+B Loans
- Structure allows commercial banks to benefit from IFC's preferred creditor status = "halo effect"
- IFC loans exempt borrower from interest withholding taxes
- IFC A Loan has longer loan tenor (+2 years) and higher pricing (+.25–.75bps) versus B Loan

STAKEHOLDER ALIGNMENT ISSUES

As previously noted, achieving solid project stakeholder alignment in relation to risk sharing, project returns (as between project investors and local community), buy-in, and government political support and local societal support is critical to the long-term sustainability and success of any project finance deal in emerging markets. The IFC's working mantra when implementing financing for high-risk emerging markets is: "If it's not fair, it's not sustainable." One of the most important lessons when working on project finance deals is to remember that financial close is not the end, it is the beginning. Infrastructure investments have a long-lived asset life of 30–40 years in most cases. For both lenders and equity investors the recovery of loan capital and equity payback and returns will take 10–20 years, and that timeframe will likely entail multiple changes of government, laws, tax rules, and regulatory policies. Projects need to ensure there is an equitable sharing of the project's economic value chain to ensure they can navigate all of these likely—but unknown—future developments.

MITIGATING POLITICAL AND SOVEREIGN RISKS

The mitigation of political and sovereign risks can take many forms, both explicit or implicit. The explicit forms of political risk mitigation include the use of ECAs, which can provide PRI cover to commercial bank lenders for the three legs of political risks—war/riots, nationalization/expropriation, and currency convertibility/transfer. ECAs require some level of risk sharing with commercial banks and as such will normally provide 85% PRI cover, with the commercial banks assuming the 15% residual, or top-up, exposure. Banks view this covered/clean exposure mix as attractive on an adjusted risk-return basis given the small absolute amount of uncovered or clean exposure and the fact that the ECA is taking most of the political risks. ECAs can also provide what is called "expanded" PRI cover, which includes the three basic legs of PRI plus commercial risk cover or breach of contract cover. The combined PRI and commercial risk cover is referred to as comprehensive cover, and ECAs generally provide a lower level of comprehensive cover (60–80%) due to expectation/requirement that banks should be able to assess and accept a material amount of project commercial risks.

Implicit forms of political risk mitigation for commercial banks include either co-financing across and among MDBs and BDBs on a direct loan basis, or via A:B loan lending programs where banks benefit from MDBs' "preferred creditor" or "halo effect" by virtue of MDBs' more protected lender status including priority access to foreign exchange and typical exclusion from sovereign defaults and debt restructuring and rescheduling.

Case Study: Dabhol Power Project, India

The Dabhol Power Project is a seminal project finance case study and a cautionary tale of the risks and challenges navigating political risks in emerging markets.[6] It is also a story of a flawed market entry strategy into India and how the deeply engrained corporate culture of hubris by the main project sponsor and the "bête noire" of energy markets and accounting rules—Enron Corporation—served to conspire to cause one of the greatest and largest project finance failures in recent living memory. The case also provides a window into how and why Enron's bankruptcy occurred in December 2001.

Project Overview and Background

Since independence in 1947, India pursued an economic policy based on protectionism, state control, and self-sufficiency. In 1992 India embarked on a series of market reforms and economic liberalizations aimed at opening key infrastructure sectors (power, rail, roads, ports, etc.) to the private sector with a view to increasing foreign direct investment. The Indian government private power initiative was based on a strategy to fast-track the first eight power projects by foregoing an open, competitive tendering process and instead negotiating bilateral deals with IPPs. The rationale was that India needed to make a statement to the international investing community that India was open for business and by fast-tracking these initial pioneering projects it would pave the way for follow-on private sector investment in infrastructure. It also reflects in part India's weak negotiating position competing for scarce capital and the need to create favorable market conditions to attract foreign investors. India also represented significant country risk for foreign investors with sub-investment-grade credit ratings, weak macroeconomic fundamentals (GDP per capita was only $371), and low foreign currency reserves (only two weeks of import cover). The investment return terms of the private power initiative launched by India were inherently flawed. India offered foreign investors a 16% return on equity (ROE) for private power projects, which achieved a minimum 68.5% plant load factor (PLF). ROE in turn is based on net worth, which is driven by project costs—effectively creating no incentive to minimize project costs.

Dabhol is a 2,015 MW, $2.8 billion gas-fired power project located 100 miles south of Mumbai in Maharashtra State, India. Maharashtra is India's third-largest state and the main commercial and industrial center of India. Originally conceived as a single project, Dabhol was subsequently divided into two phases: Phase 1 consisted of a 695 MW distillate oil-fueled power plant and phase 2 a 1,325 MW gas-fired power plant, with phase 1 also converted to gas-fired generation. The capital costs for phase 1 were $920 million with phase 2 capital costs $1.9 billion. The rationale for a 2,015 MW power plant was the LNG fuel supply to be sourced by Enron from Qatar, which would require a minimum offtake capacity of about 2,000 MW to support the economics and capital cost for the investment and construction of a single LNG train with a nameplate production capacity of 2.5 million tons of LNG.

Dabhol was developed in the mid-1990s by Enron Corporation, at the time one of the world's largest developers of greenfield energy projects in emerging markets and the largest natural gas pipeline company in the US, with revenues of $9 billion. GE and Bechtel also partnered with Enron as equity investors on the Dabhol project, with Bechtel acting as the general construction contractor and GE supplying the gas turbines for the project. Enron performed multiple project roles, including construction management, project operator, fuel supply manager, and project engineering. Dabhol had a very aggressive timeline for negotiating and signing key project documentation with India authorities—the PPA and various other key project documents were executed in December 1993, barely 15 months after Enron began investigating the possibility of undertaking a power project in India. Financial close followed in January 1995 with the project financing of $643 million provided by a consortium of international and local lenders comprising the Export-Import Bank of the US ($298 million), the Overseas Private Investment Corporation, or OPIC ($100 Million), local Indian banks ($95 million rupee loan equivalent), and international banks led by Bank of America and ABN Amro ($200 million).

(continued)

(*continued*)

Maharashtra State elections in April 1995 resulted in the nationalistic BJP party ousting the incumbent Congress Party. BJP ran on a platform of industrial nationalism and jingoistic protectionism. The BJP specifically targeted the cancellation of the Dabhol project if elected. An investigation into the Dabhol project by the BJP resulted in a decision to cancel Dabhol, and after that, project construction was put on hold. The key grievances were the high cost of power, the excessive returns that Enron was receiving (26.5% IRR), and allegations of bribery and corruption stemming from the lack of transparency of the negotiated deal and a lack of competitive bidding. Following intensive negotiations between Enron, the government of Maharashtra (GOM), and the government of India (GOI), Enron agreed to reduce its project returns to 25.5% and cut project costs (the lower project returns were largely offset by a fall in steel prices and the resulting reduction in EPC costs), and construction recommenced in January 1996. Phase 1 of Dabhol reached commercial operations in 1999.

Dabhol Project Finance Risk Analysis:

The key contractual and structural risk analysis for the Dabhol project financing are set out below:

- *Construction Risk:*
  - Fixed price, date-certain EPC contract from GE and Bechtel with LD payments for delay and performance shortfall;
  - Project cost overrun contingencies; and
  - Proven technology.
- *Revenue Risk:*
  - 20-year take or pay power purchase agreement (PPA) with the Maharashtra State Electricity Board (MSEB);
  - The GOM provided a guarantee of MSEB's payment obligations under the PPA, and the GOI in turn counter-guaranteed GOM guarantee obligations;
  - Most State Electricity Boards (SEBs) in India were technically insolvent (only two SEBs with positive ROI) due to 30% technical and non-technical losses arising from electricity theft and poor transmission and distribution line infrastructure, poor revenue collection (SEBs only achieved 78% cost recovery), and very low PLF (56%); and

- Dabhol's cost of power to MSEB was high—7.05 cents per kWh compared to average MSEB power tariff of 3.34 cents per kWh—raising a question regarding MSEB's willingness and ability to pay the power price under the PPA. The level of electricity price cross-subsidization between agricultural and residential consumers and commercial and industrial users, and MSEB's resulting failure to recover the full costs distorted the electricity price comparison with Dabhol's fully loaded cost of electricity. Dabhol was designed to operate as a base load plant and as such needed to run at 95% capacity to achieve optimal project economics; operating below 95% base load capacity results in much higher average electricity costs per kWh.

- *Political Risk:*
  - India represented material country risk due to lack of track record of foreign direct investment, sub-investment-grade sovereign credit ratings, and state versus central government conflicts (in India the state governments controlled 65% of power generation while the central government controlled 31%);
  - India had only just emerged from 40 years of economic nationalism and protectionism and had an unproven track record of economic liberalization;
  - In spite of Maharashtra State elections in April 1995 indicating that the pro-Dabhol Congress Party would cede power to the nationalistic BJP party, Enron pressed ahead with financial close and the start of construction of phase 1 of Dabhol. The arrogant failure to understand and anticipate local political sentiment was a major blind spot and proved to be an Achilles' heel for Enron;
  - While Dabhol included financing from US financial institutions (Export-Import Bank of the US and OPIC), it did not include any MDBs, such as the IFC or the ADB, which would have provided stronger political risk mitigation; and
  - The World Bank reviewed the Dabhol project and the PPA on behalf of GOM and refused to support or endorse the project citing it was "economically unviable." The World Bank's analysis determined that Dabhol's installed capacity was

(continued)

(continued)

too large, the power cost too expensive, and the agreements economically lopsided in favor of Enron. The World Bank advocated that India first undertake privatization and reform of the electricity sector aimed at de-bundling generation, transmission, and distribution and put the SEBs on a stable financial footing before proceeding with IPPs. Notwithstanding the views of the World Bank, Enron pressed ahead with the Dabhol project.

Dabhol Project Outcomes

Dabhol was beset with problems from the outset, and in retrospect it was doomed to failure. As already explained, within months of financial close in January 1995, elections in Maharashtra State resulted in the nationalist BJP party coming to power. The BJP made the cancellation of the Dabhol project a top priority, which in turn ensured the project was rendered a political football. The aggressive—and one-sided—commercial negotiations that Enron drove with the GOM and the GOI further exposed Dabhol to these heightened political and regulatory risks.

Almost immediately following commercial operations in 1999, the MSEB was struggling to make payments under the PPA due to the very high price of electricity arising from a devaluation of the Indian rupee, which increased the imported fuel costs, and the indexation of the USD-denominated PPA power tariff. MSEB delayed PPA payments during 2000 and only made payment of arrears after demand for payment by Dabhol. However, the writing was on the wall, and MSEB subsequently ceased making payments by attempting to terminate the PPA on the basis of a technicality that Dabhol had failed to achieve full base load capacity within the start-up time stipulated by the technical specifications in the PPA. Dabhol countered with threats to take legal action and/or take MSEB to international arbitration to terminate the PPA and seek full repayment for the $3 billion Dabhol investment. These events were overtaken and superseded by the collapse and subsequent bankruptcy of Enron Corporation in December 2001 (the largest corporate bankruptcy in US history at the time). Dabhol entered a four-year period of legal wrangling among project stakeholders and subsequently, in 2005, a new deal was negotiated, which saw Dabhol effectively nationalized—GE, Bechtel, and Enron exited as shareholders-to-be replaced by an Indian energy company while the international lenders were bought out by the

Indian lenders, who also agreed to a debt-for-equity swap. Dabhol to this day has been plagued by financial and technical issues (inability to secure a gas supply allocation, operational issues with the turbines, failure to secure buyers for 100% of the power, non-market power price, etc.), has failed to achieve the 95% base load production capacity, and has operated sporadically and intermittently. Dabhol meets the classic definition of a "white elephant" project.

The critical reasons for the failure of the Dabhol power project can be summarized as follows:

Enron's Aggressive Corporate Culture

Enron was an energy company, but the corporate culture was more akin to an investment bank. Project developers received bonus payments tied to executing project deals, which were then handed over to the project management team; there was no accountability for the actual economic performance of the project deals. Enron was a darling of Wall Street in the late 1990s with the share price trading at PE multiples north of 50, more in line with a technology company than a mature energy industry player. The need to beat Wall Street earnings estimates every quarter fueled a corporate culture of short-term(ism). Enron also adopted a one-size-fits-all approach to project development regardless of the cultural nuances and challenges of disparate emerging markets. For example, the company rarely took a local partner when entering new developing markets and tended to negotiate aggressive terms without regard to stakeholder alignment and a balanced and fair sharing of project returns to ensure project sustainability. The IFC's adage, "If it is not fair, it is not sustainable" was never adhered to by Enron. Enron's paltry concession in negotiations with the GOM was to reduce the companies' IRR from 26.5% to 25.5%, demonstrating an inability to fully comprehend the need for an equitable sharing of project economics among project stakeholders to ensure project sustainability. The story of Dabhol's and Enron's collapse is ultimately a familiar one of ego and hubris. Enron also did not pursue political risk mitigation strategies such as seeking a local partner or including an MDB in the finance plan.

Flawed India Entry Strategy

Dabhol's 2,015 MW large size and profile exposed the project to heightened execution, integration, and political risks. An incremental approach

(continued)

(*continued*)

by leading with a smaller project to establish a track record and maximize the chances for successful execution would have been more prudent. Enron's rationale for project size was driven by a singular natural gas strategy built around sourcing LNG from Qatar. The project economics of LNG requires long-term contracts for a single train of LNG, which is 2.5 million tons of LNG; this equates to gas supply capacity requiring a 2,000 MW power plant anchor customer. Given the large capital costs for a greenfield LNG train, it must also operate at full base load design capacity. Enron also did not pursue political risk mitigation strategies such as seeking a local partner or including an MDB in the finance plan.

Unbalanced Project Economics and Risk Allocation

Enron's IRR for Dabhol was 26.5%, well above typical equity returns in the high teens/low twenties for emerging markets project finance deals at the time. This IRR level could be viewed as excessive given that most project risks were allocated to the MSEB. The MSEB was taking revenue and dispatch risk via a firm, take or pay PPA with fixed capacity payments sized to cover fixed operating expenses as well as covering full debt service and providing a return to equity to investors regardless of actual electricity dispatch. The MSEB was also required to take foreign exchange risks on fuel cost increases as well as indexed power tariff price adjustments for changes in the USD/rupee exchange rate.

High Price of Power

Dabhol's power tariff of 7.05 cents per kWh comprised a 3.38 cents per kWh fixed capacity payment and a 3.67 cents per kWh variable energy payment. The firm capacity payment was payable by the MSEB regardless of actual electricity production and dispatch and was sized to cover Dabhol's fixed operating costs as well as pay debt service and provide a minimum return on equity to shareholders. Dabhol was designed to operate as a base load power plant running at 95% production capacity in order to achieve the lowest average cost per kWh. Due to financial difficulties and an inability to pay for the full Dabhol electricity production, MSEB's actual average dispatch was closer to 40–60%. The resulting inability to spread the fixed capacity payment across higher kWhs of power generation distorted Dabhol's average power tariff, resulting in a headline power tariff twice what would be achieved if MSEB had dispatched at the planned 90–95% base load capacity. The high level of cross-subsidization and the fact that MSEB and other SEBs only achieved 78% cost recovery, combined with the political patronage of electricity (most rural and agricultural consumers paid little or nothing for electricity consumption), served to materially understate the true cost of power generation. This put Dabhol's fully costed power tariff in stark relief to local power prices, exposed the project to politicized accusations of off-market electricity costs, and in turn opened Enron and Dabhol to insinuations of bribery and corruption.

Lack of competitive bidding:

The negotiated basis of the Dabhol project—and indeed the initial eight so-called fast-track power projects in India—only served to support the conspiracy theory narrative by the BJP and its acolytes that Enron and its partners had engaged in bribery and corruption in order to obtain what were widely regarded in the public domain as extremely favorable and generous contract terms.

Rushed/aggressive project timeline:

Enron's corporate goals to meet quarterly earnings targets resulted in an overly aggressive timetable for negotiating key project documents and implementing Dabhol to be able to book the accounting earnings from Dabhol. The rushed negotiations and the resulting lopsided nature of the project risk-return allocations in favor of Enron contributed to an inherently flawed project outcome.

- May 1992—India embarks on roadshows in major financial centers and Houston, Texas, to promote and raise awareness of the fast-track private power initiative;
- June 1992—Enron visits India and meets with various state and central government officials and scouts potential sites for a power project;
- December 1993—PPA and other key project agreements including GOM guarantees and GOI counter-guarantees signed. The guarantees protected the project against payment default by the MSEB under the PPA.
- January 1995—Financial close.

(continued)

(*continued*)

Financially Weak Offtaker

As noted, the MSEB (and pretty much all the Indian SEBs) was technically insolvent as it was only recovering 78% of its cost of power generation, transmission, and distribution from its customers and had technical and non-technical line losses approaching 30%. The World Bank identified the need to first undertake structural reform of India's SEBs by deregulating and de-bundling power generation, transmission, and distribution, improving bill collection, and reducing technical and non-technical losses so that SEBs could be put on a stronger financial footing. Clearly MSEB did not have the financial wherewithal to stand behind the 20-year power purchase obligations of a 2,015 MW USD-denominated power plant. Enron and the project lenders placed material reliance on the GOM guarantee and the GOI counter-guarantee to credit-enhance the MSEB payment risk. The failure to "look through" the PPA and other project agreements to analyze and assess Dabhol's fundamental commercial viability (versus contractual viability) ultimately proved to be a fatal due diligence error.

ENDNOTES

1. Yves Albouy and Reda Bousba, *The Impact of IPPs in Developing Countries—Out of the Crisis and into the Future* (The World Bank Group Note No. 162, December 1998).

2. Suman Babbar and John Schuster, *Power Project Finance, The Experience in Developing Countries* (The World Bank Group RMC Discussion Paper Series, Number 119, January 1998).

3. Gray R. David and John Schuster, *The East Asian Financial Crisis—Fallout for Private Power Projects* (The World Bank Group Note No. 146, August 1998).

4. Agus P. Sari, *Power Sector Restructuring and Public Benefits* (Exec Director Pelangi, Jakarta, Indonesia, 1993–1994).

5. Julie M Fraser, *Lessons from the Independent Private Power Experience in Pakistan* (Energy and Mining Sector Board Discussion Paper No. 14, May 2005).

6. Anu Bhasin, Mihir Desai, and Sarayu Srinivasan, *Enron Development Corporation: The Dabhol Power Project in Maharastra, India* (Harvard Business School, July 6, 1998).

CHAPTER 5

Sources of Financing for Emerging Markets

Designing an effective and sustainable financing plan for a project finance transaction in high-risk emerging markets is critical to the enduring success of the project. Project finance advisors spend considerable time developing and fine-tuning the finance plan along with backup options to achieve the optimal mix of financing sources that aims to deliver the lowest cost debt with minimal execution risk while providing required political risk mitigation and other risk transfer benefits. Depending on the project location, risk appetite among lenders, transaction precedents, and the relative availability or scarcity of loan capital, there are a variety of strategic approaches when developing a financing plan—however, given the bespoke nature of most project deals, they tend to be highly customized. From my own experience, there are a few general rules of thumb that should be followed:

- Engage a financial advisor or an experienced project finance bank to review draft project documents before execution to undertake a sanity check as to the bankability or financeability of the project documents. One the most common mistakes made by project sponsors is to sign project documents before determining if the documents would be bankable and acceptable to lenders. Seeking to re-open project documents after execution can prove difficult and costly as project counterparties will seek other contract concessions in return for modifying the contracts to meet minimum lender requirements;

- Pursue and develop more sources of funding than required for the finance plan to ensure competitive tension among lenders;
- Always have a backup financing plan to mitigate the execution risk as some financing sources may fall away for a variety of reasons during the due diligence process and when negotiating lending terms and conditions;
- Leverage project contractual relationships and equipment sourcing to secure financing commitments. For example, the project equipment sourcing matrix during the EPC selection process will provide valuable optionality information whereby equipment can be sourced to be able to tie financing support from that country's ECA;
- Always include requests for financing proposals from EPC companies and equipment suppliers;
- Given that the complexity, cost, execution risk, time, and resources required to reach financial close increases exponentially as the number of lenders increases, try to limit the number of lenders to no more than three, four, or five maximum. This will obviously depend on the size of the transaction being considered as well as individual lender risk and capital appetite. Remember that you will end up with the lowest common denominator of lender requirements across pricing, loan tenor, sponsor support, social and environmental conditions, and so forth, so it is important to limit the number of lenders to the extent possible and ideally choose a group of lenders with similar risk thresholds and precedent experience executing similar projects;
- Identify early in the process one large ticket lender—an ECA or MDB—with good risk and strategic appetite for the deal and seek to negotiate high-level outline terms and conditions and use this as a template to approach other lenders (commercial banks, BDBs, etc.) to provide financing proposals/commitments. This can serve to better manage and control the negotiating process on key lending terms and conditions. This could also be a "pathfinder" lender with the track record, credibility, and experience to catalyze other lenders to support the project—the Mozal project is a good example whereby the project sponsors first approached the IFC to complete basic due diligence and support the deal before approaching other lenders.

Project sponsors have a range of potential strategic and commercial objectives when designing a finance plan. Those objectives and priorities can vary from optimizing project risk transfer to minimizing sponsors' credit and political risk exposure to maximizing the dividend distribution policy to achieve the highest possible project IRR returns or seeking the most favorable tax structure. That said, the most common economic objective of project sponsors when designing a finance plan—which in part or whole addresses the other objectives—is to obtain the financing that secures the lowest cost debt with the longest loan tenor and most favorable debt repayment terms.

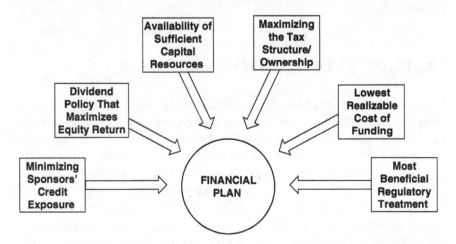

Identifying and selecting the right constituent mix of lending institutions that can work harmoniously and offer complementary synergistic value to project sponsors is key. It is also important that the lenders' risk appetite and risk assessment of the project as well as loan terms and conditions (including covenant requirements and potential sponsors support) are broadly aligned across all lenders. If there are one or more lenders with off-market lending requirements that are onerous for the project sponsors, then the loan terms for all lenders will be subject to the lowest common denominator lender. It is not uncommon for project sponsors to seek to work with the same group of lenders if they have previously worked together successfully on another project. When considering a club deal, we would generally seek out like-minded lenders we had previously worked with when putting together bank groups to bid for project finance mandates or when deciding which banks to invite to join deals as joint lead arrangers. The other consideration when selecting a lender syndicate is the execution risk and time to loan approvals. Generally, MDBs and ECAs tend to have more elongated approval processes with particularly exhaustive due diligence requirements around social and environmental risks and a more multi-layered approval process with limited flexibility to accelerate their internal approvals processes.

The other compounding issue is that some MDBs—and more typically ECAs—outsource parts of their project due diligence to outside technical consultants, which can further delay and complicate the loan approval process. Commercial banks, due in large part to close sponsor relationships, tend to be the most responsive and flexible when it comes to loan approval processes and modifying terms and conditions to meet sponsor requirements.

MULTILATERAL DEVELOPMENT BANKS (MDBS)

MDBs are global multilateral development banks, whose shareholders comprise a broad range of member sovereign countries. Examples of MDBs include the World Bank and the ADB. The IFC, the private sector arm of the World Bank, is the largest global MDB focused on lending and investing to private sector infrastructure projects in developing countries. The IFC, established in 1956, is owned by 185 member countries and governed by a board of directors. The criteria for the IFC to consider lending to a project investment are that the project ownership is private sector, there are meaningful local benefits to the host country, the project has minimal social and environmental impacts, and is commercially sound. The IFC is optimally used in high-risk countries where there are material political, legal, and regulatory risks. The IFC's preferred creditor status and membership of the World Bank serves to significantly mitigate these risks. As a result, the IFC tends to take an early stage lender pathfinder role on project deals by assisting with the contract negotiations, advising on the project structure, and conducting preliminary due diligence, particularly social and environmental due diligence. Where MDBs are included among the lenders, the debt package may benefit from certain insulation and protection from political risks. This preferred creditor status conferred on MDBs is derived from the importance of MDBs as sovereign creditors and therefore receive preferential treatment in relation to things such as access to foreign currency and exemption from capital controls. MDBs also possess leverage and access to governments to be able to more effectively resolve and negotiate any project issues that may arise. Emerging market countries are also reluctant to incur a default on a project deal involving an important MDB as it could result in the country concerned being closed out to broader MDB financing. This preferred creditor status benefits other co-financing lenders in the project financing deal—in particular, commercial banks—and is sometimes referred to as the halo effect that MDBs provide.

BILATERAL DEVELOPMENT BANKS (BDBS)

BDBs are development banks established by individual countries to finance development projects in emerging markets—hence the term "bilateral" versus "multilateral." Examples include FMO, the Dutch BDB, DEG, the Germany BDB and CDC, the UK BDB. Generally, BDBs follow similar loan processes and due diligence as MDBs—particularly in relation to social and environmental requirements. However, they tend to be more commercial, responsive, and flexible compared to the traditional MDBs. BDBs have a high emerging markets risk tolerance and can take on more challenging/complex infrastructure deals. One limitation with BDBs is that they can only typically lend small amounts per projects: $50–150 million. Therefore, the sweet spot for BDBs is smaller project deals in the $150–300 million range where they can have a more meaningful effect. BDBs provide less value added for project deals with project costs over $500 million.

EXPORT CREDIT AGENCIES (ECAS)

An ECA is a financing institution that offers to finance domestic companies' international export operations. ECAs are public agencies established by individual countries, which typically provide government-backed loans, guarantees, and insurance products. The primary role of the ECA is to support the export of goods and services from the ECA's country of domicile. ECAs currently finance or underwrite about $430 billion of business activity abroad—about $55 billion of this amount goes toward project finance in developing countries—and provide $14 billion of insurance for new foreign direct investment, dwarfing all other official sources combined.

ECA financing can take the form of direct loans, guarantees, or credit insurance guarantees depending on the mandate of the country in question. For example, the US ECA, the Export-Import Bank of the United States, offers both direct lending as well as credit insurance guarantees covering political risks—as well as commercial risks in some cases—whereas France's ECA, Coface, is solely a credit insurance agency offering guarantees for political, and sometimes commercial, risks. Most ECAs have very strict guidelines governing the quantum of the financing they can provide in that it must be directly linked or tied (referred to as "tied financing") to the amount of actual goods and services being exported from their respective countries. That said, there are several ECAs that are more flexible and able to provide "untied" financing in certain cases. Korea's KEXIM, for example, is able to consider projects that may not have direct Korean exports of goods and services but the project financing in question is deemed to be of national strategic interest. In 2013 I was involved in the financing of the $5.9 billion Sabine Pass LNG project in the US. Sabine Pass involved the export of LNG from the US to international buyers, one of whom was Korea Gas of Korea. We were able to help secure $1.5 billion of the required financing from KEXIM solely on the basis of Korea Gas's role as an offtaker and the strategic importance to Korea of securing long-term supplies of natural resources (Korea is the world's largest importer of natural gas). Other ECAs that tend to adopt a more flexible approach to export credits include the Export-Import Bank of China (CEXIM), which similar to KEXIM, can adopt a more strategic approach to financing. EDC of Canada is generally regarded by most project finance banks as the most commercially oriented and flexible in its approach to project financing, more akin to a commercial bank than an ECA.

ECAs are an attractive source of financing as they can typically provide large loan tickets—$200 million–$1 billion—subject to the project size and sourcing of equipment, goods, and services. A critical strategy in identifying potential ECA financing for project finance deals is to evaluate the equipment procurement matrix related to the proposed EPC tenders and attempt to optimize equipment sourcing from countries that offer favorable ECA financing. It is also typical to request EPC companies to submit letters of interest from the relevant ECAs when submitting their technical and commercial bids for the EPC role.

The lending terms that ECAs can offer are governed by the OECD "Consensus" guidelines, also known as the "Arrangement on Officially Supported Export Credits." The OECD Consensus is essentially a gentlemen's agreement among ECAs to abide by certain lending conditions such that there is a level playing field and no single ECA is gaining an unfair advantage by offering more favorable lending terms. The emergence of ECAs such as China's CEXIM as a significant player in the provision of export credit financing for large-scale project financings and the ability to offer untied export credits with aggressive loan terms has challenged the financial discipline that underpins the OECD Consensus. The key lending arrangements that are governed by the OECD Consensus and that all ECAs must abide by include:

- Maximum loan repayment terms offered;
- Minimum interest rates offered are set by the Commercial Reference Interest Rates (CIRR). CIRR is a set of fixed rates for each currency published on the 15th of each month and based on the prevailing AAA government bond rates.

- Minimum premium rates to cover political risks of the relevant country as well as commercial risks (if full comprehensive insurance is being offered).

COMMERCIAL BANKS

Commercial banks have traditionally played an important and consistent role in project financings due in large part to their close client banking relationships with project developers, equipment suppliers, construction companies, and project offtakers. As a result, commercial banks are typically involved in early-stage discussions with project developers and other project parties regarding project finance solutions. Project developers may mandate one bank to act as its financial advisor for the financing if the project financing is particularly challenging and complex or the sponsor has limited in-house project finance expertise. If the project developer has an in-house project finance team and has relevant experience, they may also directly issue RFPs (requests for proposals) to a number of their relationship banks to structure, arrange, and potentially underwrite and syndicate the total project financing requirement. The mandated bank or banks will then structure and negotiate the financing, and depending on the size of the deal may syndicate the financing to a broader group of banks and financial institutions. The flexibility and ability of commercial banks to play multiple roles such as financial advisor, lead arranger, provider of construction financing, working capital, and debt capital markets solutions as well as offer risk management solutions (commodity, currency, and interest rate hedging) renders commercial banks essential and central to project financing.

Project finance represents a core product offering for approximately 40–50 banks globally. European banks have historically dominated the sector and maintained a consistent focus on project financing despite the various banking crisis and cyclical economic downturns over the past 30 years. US banks have largely exited the international project finance market for long-term lending due in part to the unique nature of the US project finance market and the focus on debt capital markets. The US project finance market is largely driven by "mini-perm" project financings where banks provide short-term (5–7 years) project finance loans to fund construction financing with the bank loans refinanced in the bond markets post–construction completion when the project loan has been de-risked. Japanese banks have represented the largest share of the project finance market over the last 5 years due to a combination of low cost of funds driven by Japan's high savings rate, balance sheet size, and ability to write large take-and-hold tickets ($1 billion take-and-hold on recent US LNG deals by Japanese banks is not unusual). This market dominance is reflected in the 2019 mandated lead arranger league tables, which shows the three main Japanese banks (MUFG, SMBC, and Mizuho) representing 13.5% of the project finance market and MUFG and SMBC occupying the top two league table positions.[1] In recent years we have also seen the emergence of regional banks (such as China's Bank of China and ICBC) in Asia and Latin America as key players in the project finance market. Due to the changes in regulatory capital requirements after the 2008 financial crisis—in particular the effect of Basel III, which requires banks to set aside capital against long-term lending—the capacity for commercial banks to provide the necessary long-term project lending in emerging markets has been severely curtailed, resulting in ECAs and MDBs filling this gap in long-term commercial bank financing.

POLITICAL RISK INSURANCE MARKET—BREACH OF CONTRACT AND NON-HONORING OF FINANCIAL GUARANTEES

Political risk insurance (PRI) provides protection for project investors and lenders against political risk events by host governments and has been an important source of political risk mitigation in high-risk emerging markets. According to Gallaher's, the private insurance market for PRI is over $3.2 billion with the key private insurance underwriters being Lloyds, AIG, Axis, and Euler Hermes.[2] PRI typically covers the three points of political risk events—sovereign expropriation/nationalization; war, riots, or civil unrest; and currency convertibility and transfer risks. In the event that one or more of these risk events occurs and results in a payment default/loss to the insured lender (or project investor in the case of insured equity investment), they would have a valid claim under the PRI policy.

More recently PRI providers have expanded cover from the basic three- to four-point cover—the addition of breach of contract and non-honoring of financial obligations (NHFO) cover. NHFO cover was spearheaded by MIGA, the private insurance arm of the World Bank, and provides protection against losses resulting from a failure of a sovereign, sub-sovereign, or state-owned enterprise to make a payment when due under an unconditional financial payment obligation or guarantee related to an eligible investment. This cover effectively provides commercial credit enhancement for project finance deals where a sovereign, sub-sovereign, or state-owned enterprise is providing an unconditional payment obligation to the project. For example, a power project in Africa that has as its power purchaser under a PPA a sovereign or sub-sovereign counterparty could obtain NHFO cover for any take or pay payment defaults by the PPA offtaker. For most commercial banks this is effectively tantamount to full or comprehensive (political risk and project commercial risk) project risk cover and materially de-risks the project.

PROJECT BONDS

Project bonds are debt capital markets securities typically issued in the private placement/144A market to qualified institutional investors and can represent an attractive alternative—or complement—to bank loans. The investor base for project bonds largely comprises buy-and-hold insurance companies seeking to match long-term assets and liabilities along with pension companies, private equity, asset managers, and infrastructure debt funds. Project bond investors assume the same project finance risk as other project lenders, although they tend to favor investment grade project counterparties and infrastructure projects with fixed, take or pay, long-term offtake or availability contracts. Due to yield-chasing investors and the deep and liquid nature of the US capital markets, project bonds have increasingly become an important source of financing for project financings in the US and Europe, where investment grade credit ratings are achievable and investors are comfortable with the country risk. Bond financings are more challenging in emerging markets due to sub-investment grade sovereign credit ratings and associated political risk—although there have been good examples of project bond deals as in the case of energy and power projects in the Middle East and project bond deals in Brazil. In 2018, the US and UK represented $19 billion, or over 40% of the global project bond market. While the global project finance loan market was $283 billion in 2018, the project bond market stood at $46 billion and represented less than 20% of the corresponding project loan market. The main challenge with the project bond market is that it is a financing window that opens and closes quickly and as such is not (with the exception of the US debt capital markets) a reliable source of project financing, so it requires multiple backup financing sources. Moreover, bond investors typically shun construction risks and are more comfortable taking post-completion operational risk; at this stage the project has been materially de-risked and is more likely to achieve the required investment grade ratings sought by investors.

Bond financing provides a number of benefits to projects including lower fixed interest rates, a longer loan maturity, and more flexible amortization (which can be very helpful given the duration of most of these projects), less onerous and less restrictive covenant packages compared to bank lenders, faster execution, and more liquidity. The disadvantages associated with financing through bond issues include:

- "Negative carry." Bond financing is typically drawn all at once up front, and therefore interest is charged on the entire drawn amount from day one. The borrower will have to bear the "cost of carry," the interest paid on the bond proceeds, from the date of receipt to the date it is used to invest in capital expenditure;
- Bond investors typically require make-whole provisions in bond indentures, requiring the project to pay penalties for early prepayment of the project bond;
- Less certainty in the underwriting process due to the volatility in the securities market and resulting execution risk unless the bonds are underwritten (which is rare);
- Less flexibility during project implementation (e.g., approval of waivers and amendments), given the diversity of bondholders and the difficulty of obtaining approval for changes;
- Subject to the size and structure of the financing, credit rating requirements from at least two and typically all three major credit rating agencies are required; and
- Increased cost due to more extensive disclosure processes and the rating process.

EQUIPMENT SUPPLIERS AND FINANCING

As noted, equipment providers and EPC companies represent a critical source of potential project financing through the linking of country-of-origin equipment sourcing and potential ECA financing. It is vitally important in the early stages of selecting equipment providers and EPC contractors to scrutinize the equipment sourcing matrix detailing the countries from which the large-ticket equipment items are being sourced. It is typical to require equipment suppliers and EPC companies to provide financing letters of interest from ECAs when submitting their tender proposals. The evaluation and selection of EPC contractors should include a weighting for the quantum of potentially attractive ECA financing they can bring to the table.

INSTITUTIONAL LENDERS (INSURANCE COMPANIES, INFRASTRUCTURE FUNDS, PENSION FUNDS, PRIVATE EQUITY, AND SO FORTH)

The global infrastructure investment needs and the growing infrastructure gap is unlikely to be met with funding from traditional sources of project finance lending—banks, ECAs, MDBs, and BDBs. Institutional lenders possess the scale of capital and financing capacity to be able to solve the infrastructure funding dilemma. While project finance and infrastructure is an attractive asset class for institutional investors given the long-term matching of assets and liabilities and the superior risk-adjusted returns relative to plain vanilla corporate and government bonds, there are two main offsetting impediments for institutional investors: (1) the time-consuming, bespoke, and detailed project analysis requiring complex financial structuring and the internal deal team resources needed; and (2) the fact that institutional investors do not like construction risks and generally only participate post-completion when the project has been materially de-risked and project returns have also been reduced. Before the 2008 financial crisis, monoline insurers mitigated the first issue by providing insurance wraps and therefore taking on the project risk analysis and freeing institutional investors from this burden. In the aftermath of the 2008 financial crisis the monoline insurers exited this market, and this void has been filled by several public sector institutions such as MDBs, who started providing credit enhancement guarantee structures to bonds issued to institutional investors. Investment managers have also developed deep in-house project and infrastructure finance expertise, which has further helped mitigate this concern. The second issue has partially been addressed by the emergence of joint lending between institutional investors and banks, where banks provide shorter tenor "mini-perm" construction loans and amortize ahead of the institutional lenders, who prefer the long-dated bond tenor to better match long-term liabilities.

STRATEGIES FOR MULTI-SOURCED FINANCING IN EMERGING MARKETS

Most project finance deals in high-risk developing countries will require two or more lending institutions given the low-risk appetite and tight offshore financing capacity for the market in question. The need to tap multiple sources of financing for infrastructure projects in emerging markets necessitates a strategic approach to decision-making around which and how many lenders to approach and the timing within which to execute the finance plan. There are a few golden rules to follow:

- Try to minimize the total number of lenders in the project financing to avoid overly complicating and elongating the execution of the financing. Subject to the size of the financing, limit the number of lenders to no more than five as the rule of the lowest common denominator will apply when it comes to each lender's credit approval conditions and requirements in the final terms of the financing;
- Identify like-minded lenders with similar risk thresholds, approaches to due diligence, and expected credit approval conditions and requirements to commit to the deal;
- Identify one anchor lender (perhaps an MDB or an ECA) committing the largest loan amount to the financing and first negotiate the high-level or outline terms and conditions of the financing, and only after this has been agreed do you approach other prospective lenders with a quasi fait-accompli financing terms; and
- Always ensure you have several backup financing sources in the event that your primary source of financing falls away.

Case Study: Nam Theun 2 Hydro Project, Laos

Nam Theun 2 (NT2) is an excellent example of a successful high-risk emerging markets project deal entailing complex financial execution achieving extensive multi-sourced financing. The project involved significant social and environmental risks as well as major cross-border risks along with unique cross-currency risks, which required innovative, groundbreaking solutions. The final finance plan involved 27 different lending institutions covering the gambit of MDBs, ECAs, and BDBs along with consortiums of offshore international banks as well as onshore commercial banks. It is widely held up as a model for how to execute a successful multi-sourced financing while mitigating and overcoming significant project risks. In the aftermath of the 1997 Asian currency crisis and the lessons learned, NT2 represented a model for how project financing deals can organically mitigate currency mismatch risks by creatively aligning the currency mix across project costs, sources of financing, and project revenues. It was also a groundbreaking project for the World Bank—the largest hydroelectric dam project it has financed and the first in about 20 years—and is consistently touted as best practice for how to successfully implement these types of high-impact projects while achieving win-win outcomes for all project stakeholders. At the time of financial close, NT2 represented a number of firsts—the largest cross-border power deal in Asia, the largest internationally financed IPP in Asia since the 1997 Asian currency crisis, and the largest privately financed hydroelectric power deal in the world.

Project Overview and Background

NT2 is a 1,070 MW, $1.6 billion run-of-the-river hydroelectric power project located in Laos. About 95%, or 995 MW, of the electricity produced would be exported to neighboring Thailand under a long-term offtake agreement with EGAT, the largest power generation company in Thailand. Thailand's economy was growing rapidly with resulting electricity needs outpacing domestic power generation and requiring imports of electricity. For Laos, the $2 billion of project royalties and tax revenues from NT2 over 20 years would represent 85% of its annual GDP and would be the largest foreign currency generator and largest contributor to the government's budget. Under the supervision of the anchor lenders (World Bank and the ADB), Laos was subject to an innovative revenue sharing agreement under which the $2 billion of Laos government revenues over the operational life of NT2 would be dedicated to poverty reduction and economic development. Laos and Thailand have a long history of cross-border electricity sales, having commenced power trading in the early 1970s with total electricity sales from Laos to Thailand representing over 3,000 MW at the time NT2 was developed. NT2 was 30 years in the making having been initially conceived in the mid-1970s with pre-feasibility studies conducted with the assistance of the World Bank. However, it was not until the early 1990s that NT2 moved to the development phase following the identification of the project sponsors and the support of the World Bank to provide financing. The 1997 Asian currency crisis forced the project to be placed on hold, and it was only resurrected again in early 2000. The key project agreements and contracts were negotiated and executed in 2002–2003 with financial close following in 2005. The key project sponsor was EDF International (EDFI), a

(*continued*)

(*continued*)

subsidiary of the national French electric utility Électricité de France. EDFI assumed multiple roles on NT2 including the largest shareholder with 35% equity, lead construction contractor (managing three major subcontractors and two electric-mechanical subcontractors), as well as project operator. The other major shareholders were EGCO (25%), a Thai power generation company; Government of Laos (GOL, 25%); and an Italian private power company (15%). Two 25-year PPAs were executed with EGAT for 95% of the electricity production with the remaining 5% contracted to the Laos national utility, EdL.

NT2 Project Finance Risk Mitigation

The key project risks and corresponding mitigation measures were as follows:

- *Construction Risk*—Mitigated as follows:
  - Key sponsor EDFI assumed construction risk via a fixed-price, date-certain EPC contract. This was unprecedented as most hydro projects involve significant local civil works and material sub-surface geotechnical risks, which most EPC contractors are not prepared to fully wrap;
  - Project cost overrun contingencies, and
  - Proven technology and successful track record and credibility of EDFI developing and implementing large-scale hydro power projects in challenging emerging markets.
- *Revenue and Hydrology Risk*—Mitigated as follows:
  - Key project revenue contract is 25-year take or pay PPA with EGAT for 995 MW, or 95% of power production; 5%, or 75MW, sold to EdL;
  - PPAs conservatively based on primary energy production with tariff and payment 50% USD/Thai baht so that tariff currency split matches debt financing;
  - NT2 provides very low cost of power (2.11 cents/kWh) to EGAT, providing a strong commercial incentive to perform under PPA;
  - Hydrology risk mitigated by 30-year hydrology records, energy production in PPA sized conservatively at minimum

annual hydrology production over last 30 years and water storage reservoir capacity;

- EGAT controls project electricity dispatch. Innovative "energy banking" structure does not require EGAT to dispatch all energy production but requires minimum energy payment, which smooths out hydrology impact and ensures a stable cash flow stream to NTPC. Where EGAT dispatches less than minimum payment, EGAT effectively "banks" a future energy credit for energy dispatch shortfall; and

- EGAT's PPA structure, which mitigated hydrological risk, includes separation of its energy purchase and payment obligations. It also incorporated a split tariff structure. This unique and complex structure, together with the large storage capability of the reservoir, gives NTPC the maximum opportunity to stabilize its revenues and significantly reduce its (and the lenders') exposure to any variations in hydrological conditions.

- *Currency Risk*—Mitigated as follows:
  - NT2 created an innovative structure to align currency mix between project costs, financing sources, and offtake revenues; and
  - Project costs constituted 63% foreign currency and 37% local currency while the project capital structure across debt and equity funding comprised 64% foreign currency and 36% Thai baht local currency financing while the PPA revenue mix was 50:50 US dollars and Thai baht denominated. This helped create a natural currency mismatch hedge for the project lenders.

- *Environmental and Social (E&S) Risk*—Mitigated as follows:
  - E&S risks were significant given the nature of hydroelectric projects, which required the construction of a 450 sq. km dam and reservoir and the resettlement of over 6,000 people from 15 villages including over 40,000 people downstream whose fishing livelihood was affected as well as biodiversity and endangered-species impact from the dam construction and associated deforestation;
  - The concession agreement between the GOL and the project company (NTPC) included provisions and commitments for

(continued)

(*continued*)

E&S risk mitigation, specifically $100 million to mitigate E&S risks during construction and a further $60 million to address resettlement and livelihood improvement as well as watershed management and biodiversity remediation during the concession period;

- The World Bank and the ADB were key to conducting rigorous E&S due diligence and designing the required mitigation and monitoring plan; and
- NT2 had a net positive environmental effect by virtue of negating the need for EGAT to have to construct an equivalent gas-fired power generation project in Thailand, thus saving 2,000 tons of CO_2 in annual greenhouse gas emissions.

- *Financial Structure*—Conservative:
  - 72:28 debt-to-equity ratio and robust minimum and average DSCRs;
  - Financing included senior debt facilities of $1.132 billion equivalent, denominated in Thai baht and US dollars, with shareholder equity commitments of $450 million. 27 financial institutions participated in the financing, including the World Bank, ADB, EIB (EIB), MIGA, Nordic Investment Bank, Coface, EKN, GIEK, Agence Française de Développement (AFD), Proparco, Thai-Exim, and 16 Thai and international commercial banks;
  - ECAs, World Bank, MIGA, and ADB provided PRI guarantees to commercial banks—covers war/riots, expropriation, currency convertibility/transfer, and breach of contract;
  - Laos subject to revenue management agreement—project proceeds applied to poverty reduction/education projects; and
  - Back-ended equity funding enhanced IRR returns to project sponsors.

- *Political Risk*—Mitigated as follows:
  - The contractual structure was developed under two aspects: first, to ensure that Thai political risks were satisfactorily addressed under the PPA with EGAT, in accordance with the

framework established by Thai IPP financings, and second, that the GOL political risks were allocated to the government under the concession agreement consistent with precedents for emerging market projects;

- High value project to Thailand—NT2 is a low-cost power producer positioned atop Thailand's merit order dispatch ahead of fossil-fueled power generation. With respect to potential Thai political risks, the highly attractive tariff of approximately $2.11/kWh meant that EGAT would enjoy sustained economic advantages from the PPA, thus reducing the risks of breach of contract.;

- Comfort was also drawn from the unbroken 30-year history of cross-border power sales between Laos and Thailand and the memorandum of understanding (MOU) covering 5,000 MW of electricity exchanges between the countries;

- Multi-sourced financing comprising 27 global financial institutions across MDBs, BDBs, ECAs, and offshore and local Thai banks materially reduced political risks. The involvement of all the major Thai commercial banks and Thai-Exim added a further level of reassurance to the non-Thai lending parties; and

- Importance of NT2 and financial benefits to Laos—GOL 25% equity ownership interest in NT2 and $2 Billion of future royalty and tax revenues over 25-year concession period created strong incentive to support project and stakeholder alignment.

Nam Theun 2 Project Outcomes

NT2 achieved financial close in 2005 with construction completion and start of commercial operation achieved on budget and schedule in 2010. The $1.1 billion multi-source finance plan comprised 27 lenders including three MDBs (World Bank, ADB, and NIB), four ECAs (Coface of France, EKN of Sweden, GIEK of Norway, and Thai-Exim, Thailand's ECA), two BDBs (Proparco of France and the EIB) along with nine international banks and seven Thai commercial banks.

(*continued*)

(continued)

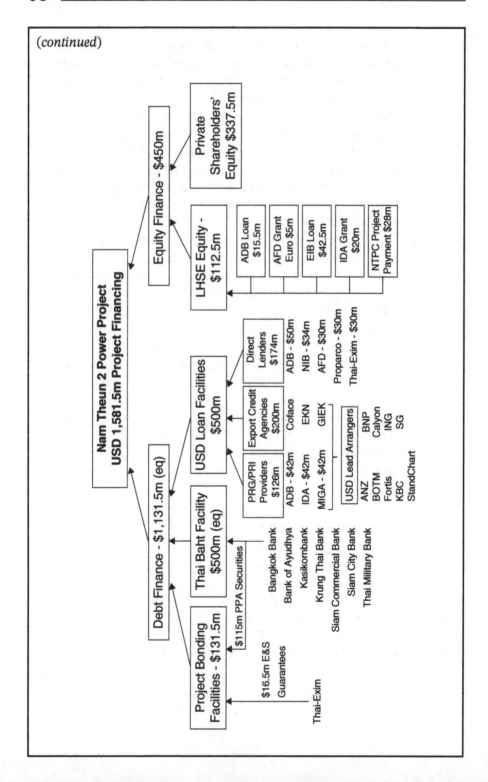

NT2 also delivered significant positive macroeconomic outcomes for Laos. Since the start of commercial operations in 2010, NT2 has consistently met its energy production targets, and the GOL has received about $174 million in gross revenues from NTPC. The project delivered livelihood, health, and education benefits for over 6,000 resettled people on the Nakai Plateau. Specifically, resettled families are benefitting from: 1,310 new houses with bathrooms and toilets, electricity, and rainwater collection tanks; 330 water pumps; 270 kilometers of new or upgraded access roads; 16 nurseries and 17 primary schools, two new health centers, and an upgraded district hospital; and community infrastructure such as roofed markets. Resettled families also received financial and technical support to take advantage of new livelihood opportunities. A household survey conducted in 2013 found that over 86% of resettled families reported they were better off than before resettlement and that 97% of resettled families had reached the "Household Income Target"—the Laos national rural poverty line[3]. A later survey, conducted in 2014, confirmed that the average consumption of resettled communities significantly exceeds the rural average. In 2014, a GOL decree was signed confirming that household income targets for Nakai district had been achieved in accordance with the concession agreement. Before the project, most settlers were below the poverty line—now 97% were above the poverty line with average consumption levels three times those before resettlement without any increase in household debt. 87% of resettled families described life as better than before resettlement. Child mortality has dropped to 50 per 1,000 from 120 per 1,000. The incidence of parasitic infection is down to 21% of the population from 60% before. Today, 90% of children on the Nakai Plateau aged 5 to 9 are attending primary school, up from 37% before the project.

ENDNOTES

1. Refinitiv, *Global Project Finance Review* (Full Year 2019).
2. Gallagher, *Structured Credit and Political Risk Insurance, Report and Update* (Jan. 2020), 16.
3. Nam Theun 2 Press Release, *"Nam Theun 2 Resettlers Have Exceeded the Household Income Target"* (July 23, 2014).

CHAPTER 6

Financial Structuring and Debt Sizing

Project financing constitutes a large and complex set of interdependent and interlocking project contracts and financing documents that must function and operate harmoniously and seamlessly. The quantitative distillation of these contracts and documents is reflected in the project financial model. The financial model is a critical feature of project finance due diligence used to determine the economic feasibility of the project and the mutual basis on which both lenders and sponsors test project assumptions and variables and ultimately agree on the debt financing terms and conditions. As such, the accuracy of the financial model is key—in particular, the input assumptions that form the basis of the economic outputs. These financial model economic outputs are deterministic in defining the ability of project cash flows to comfortably support the pro forma project leverage under all projected circumstances as well as the appropriate loan amortization profile. This is reflected in the relationship between project free cash flows and debt service (annual loan principal and interest payments) captured in the annual debt service coverage ratio (ADSCR) as well as the equity metrics (IRR, NPV, and payback period) for sponsors. In most project finance deals, the sponsors will have initially developed a "sponsor equity" financial model, which will be sponsor-friendly in the sense that it has optimistic/upside equity assumptions and features. When project lenders are initially brought into the deal, they may elect to use the sponsor model and revise and repurpose it to reflect lenders' more conservative base case and downside assumptions and

101

scenarios or, alternatively, decide to build a lender financial model from scratch. Once the lender base-case financial model has been agreed, lenders will perform a number of downside sensitivity analysis cases (for example, a 10% increase in operating expenses, a 20% decline in project revenues, or a 15% increase in interest rates) as well as combined downside cases to assess the robustness of the project case flows to be able to service the debt under all stress-case scenarios. Typically, project lenders run financial model downside sensitivity analysis for:

- Construction delays/cost overruns;
- Reduced prices or lower availability;
- Break-even prices;
- Higher input costs;
- Higher operating expenses;
- Higher interest rates; and
- Combination scenario.

On most project deals, a financial modeling bank is selected; this bank is solely responsible for preparing and controlling the master financial model, and any subsequently agreed changes in order to ensure consistency, transparency, and integrity is maintained throughout the entire financing process. Financial models are complex and error prone. Financial model errors (poor design or mistakes such as incorrect cell references, incorrect formulas, linking wrong cell) or input assumptions inconsistent with project documents and financing terms or inadequate flexibility (hard-coded assumptions in formula, which do not change with change in assumptions or did not model a contract obligation) are not unusual. As a result, lenders will normally require a financial model audit by a reputable accounting firm as a precondition to financial close to check the model for tax and accounting assumptions as well as any errors or mistakes.

The financial model is typically constructed using large Excel spreadsheets with multiple linked input and output sheets, the key ones being:

- Data input and assumptions—contains key project assumptions and ability to change input cells that drive revenues and expenses to observe effect on model outcomes;
- Capital costs (construction)—details the drawdown and funding sequence by both debt and equity for construction costs during the construction period;

- Insurance;
- Taxes;
- Depreciation;
- Financing;
- Income statement;
- Balance sheet;
- Cash flow—key worksheet, which details project cash flow ability to service or cover debt service;
- Retained earnings;
- Coverage ratios—details key lender model outcomes; and
- IRR, present values—details key sponsor model outcomes.

Project finance models are typically used before financial close to evaluate a project's financial aspects and develop a lender's base case, undertake lender due diligence, quantitatively capture and reflect the agreed contractual obligations among all project parties, assist with formulating financial provisions in the project contracts, and finally, structure the financing and evaluate pros and cons of different financing sources for sponsors. After financial close the model is used as a budgeting tool as well as a basis for lenders to assess any project waiver or amendment requests to the project contracts and documents and to be able to review changes in project performance and changes to financing terms.

THE BORROWER/SPONSOR OBJECTIVES

Project sponsors have a wide range of strategic, commercial, and economic objectives when designing and selecting the finance plan and the debt structuring. These objectives and their relative priority vary from maximizing risk transfer to the project company to optimizing the tax structure and dividend distributions to achieve the highest IRR. Ultimately most sponsors focus on achieving the highest possible leverage with the lowest cost debt and longest loan tenor. There is an obvious trade-off between maximizing leverage and loan terms and project risk transfer—the more aggressive the capital structure and the more risk assumed by the project company, the more lenders will seek higher levels of contingent sponsor support, which in turn shifts some risks back onto the sponsors. Execution risk is another key concern of sponsors, and as such they will typically want to ensure they have a primary finance plan as well as backup options. This not only ensures there are contingency plans should one lender fall away, but it also ensures competitive tension is maintained among lenders and sponsors are not held to ransom by the lowest common denominator lender requirements.

LENDERS' OBJECTIVES

Unlike project sponsors, lenders do not participate in any upside performance by the project company. The best case for lenders is that their loans get repaid on schedule and in full. Lenders are only concerned with the downside risk of project underperformance and the ability of the project cash flows to service the debt and ultimately ensure repayment of the project loan(s). As noted, project finance is a form of contract-based cash flow lending and not asset-based lending. Hence, lenders are acutely focused on the strength of the project contracts and related counterparty creditworthiness along with the robustness and sustainability of the project cash flows underpinning these contracts. The key metric governing the relationship between project cash flows and debt (principal and interest) service that project lenders focus on is the ADSCR. The ADSCR is defined as the quotient between cash flows available for debt service and debt service and is expressed as a ratio. For example, if the ADSCR for a project finance deal is 2.0x, it indicates that for every dollar of debt service there are two dollars of free cash flow available to cover or service this debt. It effectively illustrates the quantum of "cash flow cushion," which can absorb downside project performance from the lenders' base case (decline in project revenues, increase in operating costs, higher interest rates, etc.).

DEBT SIZING AND SCULPTING

Lenders are primarily concerned that the leverage or debt level is appropriate for the underlying project cash flows and that there is a robust ability of the project cash flows to service the loan repayment under a myriad of lender base-case and downside scenarios. The two interlocking metrics that drive the determination of the appropriate leverage and debt capacity for any project financing are the debt-to-equity ratio (or leverage ratio) and the ADSCR. For higher risk projects, such as natural resource projects taking commodity price risk with less predictable and more volatile cash flow streams, the leverage will be lower, and the lender ADSCR requirement will be higher. Conversely, a power project with a firm take or pay offtake contract with no volume or price risk and stable, predicable cash flows would support higher leverage and a lower minimum lender ADSCR requirement. While designing and setting the debt capacity and ADSCR is driven by the unique and specific risk and contractual aspects of each project deal, the broad rule of thumb for leverage and minimum ADSCR across a spectrum of project types and risk profiles is as follows:

1. Projects with stable project cash flows and firm take or pay offtake contracts (power projects)
   - 80:20–90:10 debt-to-equity ratio
   - 1.20x–1.25x minimum ADSCR
2. Projects with some market or revenue risk (toll roads with limited traffic risk)
   - 80:20–70:30 debt-to-equity ratio
   - 1.30x–1.40x minimum ADSCR
3. Projects with full commodity price risk exposure (oil and gas or petrochemical projects)
   - 70:30–60:40 debt-to-equity ratio
   - 1.50x–1.75x minimum ADSCR
4. Projects with full market risk and no offtake contract (merchant power projects)
   - 60:40–50:50 debt-to-equity ratio
   - 1.80x–2.00x minimum ADSCR

Small changes in the minimum required ADSCR can have disproportionately large effects on the debt capacity of a project financing. As the table below illustrates, a change in the ADSCR from 1.25x to 1.40x decreases the debt capacity and leverage for the project from $30,424 to $27,161.

Minimum DSCR and Debt Capacity		
Loan tenor	15	
Interest rate	8%	
Annual free cash flow (a)		$5,000
Annual debt service coverage ratios (b)	1.25	1.40
Maximum annual debt service = (a)/(b)	$4,000	$3,571
Maximum debt	$30,424	$27,161

By increasing the target ADSCR, we reduce the debt repayments in each but the later repayment periods. This effectively delays or back-ends the loan repayment profile, which is normally desirable for the sponsor as it increases the sponsors' IRR. There will be a limit or upper cap to the ADSCR that the project can accommodate, since the debt still needs to be repaid within the set loan tenor. Conversely, a lower ADSCR target increases the debt repayments in each period, which leads to the debt being repaid earlier and the project IRR being lower.

FINANCIAL STRUCTURING—DEBT SIZING AND LOAN AMORTIZATION

A critical skillset in project financing is the ability to manipulate the financial model to structure and design the optimal debt sizing capacity and loan amortization profile that addresses lenders' requirements to ensure there is sufficient debt service capacity under all base-case and downside scenarios while meeting sponsors' objectives to maximize project IRR. The loan repayment or loan amortization profile in project finance deals is typically mortgage or annuity style semi-annual loan repayments versus equal or level semi-annual loan repayments. The reason for using an annuity style repayment profile is illustrated by the following simple financial model example based on the input assumptions below:

- Annual project cash flows: $20 million
- Project costs: $125 million
- Project loan amount: $100 million (80%)
- Sponsor equity: $25 million (20%)
- Interest rate: 8%
- Loan tenor: 10 years

Under an equal annual loan repayment profile as illustrated in the following table, the ADSCR would increase over time as the loan amount is reduced. In year 1, for example, the ADSCR is only 1.11x, which is extremely tight and exposes the project company to a potential technical loan default should project cash flows be less than projected in the initial year of project start-up and/or project costs exceed projections. The critical period for most projects is the initial ramp-up years of commercial operations after construction completion when most projects experience operational, technical, or contractual teething issues before a stable steady-state operational performance is established. According to an S&P study, 75% of all project finance loan defaults occur in the first 4–5 years. Hence, lenders (and sponsors) generally like to see the ADSCR at its most robust in the initial years after completion.

Effects of Level Principal Payments on DSCR and IRR											
Year	0	1	2	3	4	5	6	7	8	9	10
(a) Project cash flow		20	20	20	20	20	20	20	20	20	20
Lenders' viewpoint											
(b) Loan repayments		10	10	10	10	10	10	10	10	10	10
(c) Loan outstanding	100	90	80	70	60	50	40	30	20	10	0
(d) Interest payments		8	7.2	6.4	5.6	4.8	4	3.2	2.4	1.6	0.8
(e) Total debt service = (b)+(d)		18	17.2	16.4	15.6	14.8	14	13.2	12.4	11.6	10.8
ADSCR = (a)/(e)		1.11	1.16	1.22	1.28	1.35	1.43	1.52	1.61	1.72	1.85
Average life of loan	5.5										
Investors' viewpoint											
Equity investment	25										
Dividends = (a) – (e)	−25	2	2.8	3.6	4.4	5.2	6	6.8	7.6	8.4	9.2
NPV of investments	4.00										
IRR (%)	13.9										
Payback period (yrs.)	6.1										

Taking the same project assumptions and instead applying a mortgage annuity–style loan amortization, we can achieve a more consistent and robust project ADSCR of 1.34x in each year. While the average life of the loan is extended from 5.5 years under an equal repayment profile to 6.6 under the annuity amortization profile, this is preferential to lenders as it results in a better matching of project cash flows to total debt service. Annuity-style loan repayments also benefit the project sponsor as the equity payback period is lowered from 6 years to 5 years and the IRR increases from 13.9% to 16.6%.

Effects of Annuity Payments on DSCR and IRR											
Year	0	1	2	3	4	5	6	7	8	9	10
(a) Project cash flow		20	20	20	20	20	20	20	20	20	20
Lenders' viewpoint											
(b) Loan repayments		7	7	8	9	9	10	11	12	13	14
(c) Loan outstanding	100	93	86	78	69	59	49	38	26	14	0
(d) Interest payments		8	7	7	6	6	5	4	3	2	1
(e) Total debt service = (b)+(d)		15	15	15	15	15	15	15	15	15	15
ADSCR = (a)/(e)		1.34	1.34	1.34	1.34	1.34	1.34	1.34	1.34	1.34	1.34
Average life of loan	6.1										
Investors' viewpoint											
Equity investment	25										
Dividends = (a) − (e)	−25	5	5	5	5	5	5	5	5	5	5
NPV of investments	5										
IRR (%)	16.6										
Payback period (yrs.)	5										

In many project finance transactions, the project cash flows are not firm or fixed but vary from period to period. For instance, an oil and gas project with commodity price risk produces a vastly different cash flow profile over time compared to a power project with a firm take or pay offtake contract. For projects involving commodity price risk that produce more volatile streams of cash flow, we typically apply what is referred to as a sculpted loan amortization profile. To put it simply, to improve the debt carrying capacity of the project, the total debt service in each period is matched to the projected CFADS such that a targeted, stable ADSCR is produced. This matching of CFADS to debt service is termed sculpting. When we sculpt debt, we are manipulating the principal repayments so that total debt service matches CFADS, and in turn, the ADSCR will follow a target profile. This exercise goes hand in hand—but is different from—the debt sizing. Debt can be sculpted by manually entering the principal to be repaid in each period using the following Excel formula: Loan Repayment = CFADS / target DSCR – interest payments. In the example below of a more volatile cash flow stream typical of natural resource project, we have set a targeted ADSCR of 1.35x such that in year 1 we derive the loan repayment amount to achieve a 1.35x ADSCR as 20/1.35 – 8 = 7. Sculpting is an effective way to ensure that loan repayments increase during periods of high project cash flows and lenders share in this upside while loan repayments are adjusted downward when commodity prices are low and the resulting project cash flows are reduced.

Effect of Sculpted Payments on DSCR and IRR											
Year	0	1	2	3	4	5	6	7	8	9	10
(a) Project cash flow		20	25	10	15	35	20	17	15	20	25
Lenders' Viewpoint											
(b) Loan repayments		7	11	1	5	20	10	9	8	12	17
(c) Loan outstanding	100	93	82	81	77	57	47	38	30	17	0
(d) Interest Payments		8	7	7	7	6	5	4	3	2	1
(e) Total debt service = (b)+(d)		15	19	7	11	26	15	13	11	15	19
ADSCR = (a)/(e)		1.35	1.35	1.35	1.35	1.35	1.35	1.35	1.35	1.35	1.35
Average life of loan	6.2										
Investors' viewpoint											
Equity investment	25										
Dividends = (a) – (e)	−25	5	6	3	4	9	5	4	4	5	6
NPV of investments	6										
IRR (%)	17.2										
Payback period (yrs.)	4.8										
Interest rate	8%										
Payments	10										
Loan	100										

LENDER RATIOS FOR DEBT CALIBRATION AND STRESS TESTING

Project lenders conduct financial modeling downside stress testing to understand a project's ability to withstand scenarios where the project's technical, operational, and financial performance falls below the lenders' base-case scenario. Downside stress–testing scenarios usually involve unexpected revenue shortfalls (lower price or volume or both for project output), project expenses exceeding base case, operational performance shortfalls, higher interest rates, and so forth. Project lenders will also conduct a combined downside scenario to determine a project's ability to withstand simultaneous multiple stress test events while still being able to meet the debt service payment obligations and avoiding an event of default. For mining and metal as well as oil and gas projects with commodity price market risk, lenders will also analyze the break-even commodity price at which the ADSCR = 1.0x. This provides a strong indicator of a project's relative ability to withstand historic low commodity prices. Also, for mining and metals and other natural resource projects (petrochemicals and refining), lenders will also evaluate the relative position of the project on the cost curve compared to all other comparable competing projects in operation: lenders usually want to see that the project they are considering financing is in the lower quartile of the global cost curve.

CASH TRAPS AND SWEEPS

Cash traps and sweeps are another form of financial engineering used in project finance models to address uncertainty or unpredictability concerning the timing and/or quantum of project cash flows. In projects with commodity price risk, lenders might seek to capture a share of any upside windfall project cash flows arising from an extremely high commodity price environment. This can be a sensitive issue for project sponsors, who regard these windfall gains as pure equity upside returns for taking the equity risk and should not be shared with senior lenders. A typical resolution might provide for any excess cash flows above an agreed upper ADSCR be shared, say, 60:40

or 75:25 between sponsors and lenders such that the lenders' 40 or 25% share would be applied toward debt prepayment. Cash traps and sweeps are also used to address issues such as dividend distribution tests where the actual ADSCR is below the ADSCR required to pay out dividends to sponsors from the dividend distribution account. Given this may be the result of an anomaly in the project performance and cash flow generation for the relevant 6-month period in question, it is market practice to allow the project company another 6 months to achieve and meet the ADSCR dividend distribution test. If the ADSCR falls below the required ADSCR for two or three consecutive periods and the project fails to meet the dividend distribution test, then the cash flows built up in the distribution account are typically applied to prepay the lenders senior debt—usually in inverse order of maturity. Cash traps and sweeps can also be used to address situations where sponsors are seeking a balloon payment of, say, 20–30% at the end of the loan tenor from lenders to improve the sponsors' IRR. This might be based on the belief and expectation on the part of the sponsor(s) that the relevant offtake contract will be renewed or an alternative offtake contract secured. This is something seen with respect to the offshore drilling rig market whereby an O&G company would enter into, say, a 10-year charter contract with an option to renew for another 10 years at offtaker's discretion. Most of these drilling rig deals were financed with balloon payments in the final year of the 10-year loan. To address the contract renewal risk, project lenders might agree to the 20–30% balloon payment subject to a requirement that all excess cash flows after debt service and available for distribution be swept into an escrow account beginning in, say, year 7 such that the amounts built up in the escrow account are sufficient to repay the balloon payment in year 10 should the charter contract not be renewed. Another structural mechanism to address unpredictable project cash flows without setting mandatory loan repayments so high as to risk triggering a project company payment default would be to have both a firm minimum periodic mandatory debt repayment amount as well as a target debt repayment amount such that failure to make the target debt repayment would not trigger a default, but this amount would get rolled forward to the next repayment period. This is a useful structure to allow lenders to capture unexpected upside or windfall project cash flows typical of natural resource projects.

Case Study: Sabine Pass LNG Project and USA-Asia Energy Flows

The Sabine Pass LNG (SPL) project is an excellent example of financial structuring and execution that resulted in one of the single largest and most innovative project financings in the last 10 years. The ground-breaking financing for SPL leveraged the existing "mini-perm" structures unique to US financial markets, which allows borrowers to raise short-term or mini-perm financing for long-term projects in the bank market and refinance these bank loans in the US debt capital markets after construction completion. SPL was one of the first projects to receive an investment grade credit rating with material construction risk and one of the few occasions where bond investors assumed (partial) construction risk. SPL was a trailblazing project that opened the project finance market for several similarly large US LNG project financings.

Project Overview and Background

SPL is a four-train, $5.9 billion LNG project financing with total project costs of around $12 billion. Total LNG production capacity from the four trains amounted to 22 million tons per annum (mtpa). SPL would go on to ultimately become a 6-train, 30 mtpa LNG capacity project with train 5 and 6 financed separately. In the late 2000s, the US was considered to be facing a shortfall in natural gas supply as US gas reserves and production declined, with an expected need to import significant volumes of LNG from the international gas markets to balance supply with expected demand. LNG is a technology that essentially chills or cools down natural gas at −260 degrees Fahrenheit and turns it into a liquid form (LNG is 1/600 the volume of gaseous-state natural gas), which can then be efficiently transported on specialized LNG tankers across oceans to end markets. In 2005, Houston-based oil and gas company Cheniere Energy raised project finance debt to construct an LNG import terminal. Within less than 5 years the US went from being natural gas deficient to becoming the world's largest oil producer and the world's second-largest natural gas producer. Unexpected success developing unconventional shale gas reserves had reversed the natural gas demand/supply situation.

Due to the sudden shift in US natural gas market fundamentals from being a gas importer to overnight becoming a major gas exporter, Cheniere Energy changed tack and embarked on developing the Sabine Pass terminal to add LNG export liquefaction services. Adding liquefaction capabilities would transform the Sabine Pass terminal into the world's first bidirectional facility, capable of liquefying and exporting domestic natural gas in addition to importing and re-gasifying foreign-sourced LNG. In 2011, SPL became the first LNG exporter to secure US Department of Energy approval for a 5-train LNG export project, and in May 2013, SPL secured $5.9 billion in project finance loans from a bank syndicate ($4.4 billion) and Korea Export Import Bank (KEXIM) ($1.5 billion) to finance the construction of the first 4 LNG trains that had secured long-term offtake contracts.[1]

Project Overview and Background

SPL was designed and permitted to construct up to four liquefaction trains, each with a nominal production capacity of 4.5 mmtpa. SPL represents a "brownfield" development project as it utilizes existing infrastructure at the Sabine Pass Terminal, thus reducing complexity, risk, and the scope of construction works. This generated substantial cost savings vis-à-vis a comparable, new greenfield LNG development. SPL secured long-term, 20-year take or pay offtake contracts (referred to as an LNG Sales and Purchase Agreement, or SPAs) with four separate offtakers for each train—BG (now owned by Shell), Spanish energy company Gas Natural, Gas Authority of India (GAIL), and Korea Gas. Under the SPAs, the offtakers pay 115% of the final settlement price for the New York Mercantile Exchange Henry Hub natural gas futures contract for the month in which the relevant cargo is scheduled, as well as a fixed sales charge for the annual quantity contracted, of $2.25–2.49 per MMBtu irrespective of whether any LNG is lifted. The project revenues from the fixed sales charges alone amount to over $2.9 billion per annum of firm, committed, take or pay cash flows from strong, creditworthy offtakers. The SPAs represented approximately 88% of the total LNG production capacity of SPL; Cheniere planned to market the balance of production capacity under short-term LNG spot trading contracts. These potential merchant revenues were not included in the lenders' base-case financial model.

The EPC contract for SPL was a lump-sum, turnkey contract with Bechtel group. Bechtel is one of the largest privately owned construction

(*continued*)

(*continued*)

companies in the world and one of the most experienced LNG construction companies, responsible for building about 30% of the existing global LNG capacity. Construction of all 4 trains was completed on budget and ahead of schedule with train 1 entering commercial operation in 2016 followed by train 2 and train 3 in 2017 and train 4 in 2018. The proven liquefaction technology employed is the ConocoPhillips Optimized Cascade® LNG Process, which was first used at the ConocoPhillips Petroleum Kenai plant built by Bechtel in 1969 in Kenai, Alaska.

The $5.9 billion project financing for SPL closed in May 2013 and comprised a $4.4 billion, 7-year mini-perm bank loan and a similar $1.5 billion, 7-year mini-perm loan from KEXIM. I was involved in the advisory team that secured the KEXIM loan, which was provided based on the Korea Gas SPA offtake and the strategic importance of securing long-term supplies of natural resources for South Korea (South Korea is the largest importer of natural gas in the world). The 7-year mini-perm structure of the financing introduced significant refinancing risks as the construction period for SPL was about 4–5 years, which only provided 2–3 years of operational cash flows—thereby resulting in minimal loan repayment and a 92% balloon payment at the end of year 7. While the project loan had a 7-year door-to-door loan tenor, the loan repayment profile was based on an 18-year fully amortizing loan given the 20-year SPA offtake contracts. The finance strategy was to use the bank loans to fund construction costs and then refinance the bank loans in the US debt capital markets during the construction period. Lenders ultimately got comfortable with the bank refinancing risk on the basis that SPL had 20-year offtake contracts with firm, stable cash flows. Should SPL be unable to achieve the necessary bank refinancing by the end of year 7, a term out analysis showed that the bank loans could be repaid in full within 5 years by sweeping all cash flows from the SPAs. Thus, the worst case was that the 7-year bank loan would convert to become a 12-year loan based on the term out analysis. The equity for SPL was provided by an investment of $2 billion from the Blackstone Group and Temasek with the balance of the $10 billion of project costs funded via cash flows during construction from early start-up of trains 1 and 2.

Project Risks Mitigation

The analysis of the key project risks and mitigation factors for the SPL project are as follows:

Construction Risks:

Fixed price, date-certain EPC contract with Bechtel. Bechtel is the largest and most experienced LNG construction contractor in the world. The brownfield expansion nature of project utilizing existing infrastructure (storage tanks, marine berths for LNG tankers, etc.) materially reduced construction risks.

Brownfield expansion—Materially reduced construction costs and risks and made SPL more cost competitive relative to comparable greenfield LNG projects. SPL projects costs were $610 per ton per annum (tpa) compared to average global greenfield LNG projects costs of $1,500–2,000 tpa due to SPL using existing marine jetties and storage tank, which can represent up to 50% of total liquefaction costs.[2]

Offtake Revenue Risk

20-year take or pay sales and purchase agreements backed by strong investment grade counterparties, who are also large actors in the gas market and with extensive experience in LNG.
The absence of destination clauses and the option available to the LNG offtakers under the SPAs not to lift the full LNG volumes and to just pay capacity charges provide the offtakers with optionality value, flexibility, and protection, strengthening the project.

Project Economics

Conservative capital structure with 60:40 debt-to-equity ratio. Average DSCR in the base case was 2.43x without assuming any LNG sales that are uncontracted. Average DSCR at 1.93x based on take or pay reservation fee payment and assuming no LNG volumes are lifted or offtaken.

Commercial Rationale: First mover advantage—SPL was the first LNG export project to secure DOE approvals.

(continued)

(*continued*)

LNG cost and supply flexibility—US-landed natural gas-indexed LNG to Europe and Asia is more competitive compared to oil-indexed LNG supplies from the Middle East. SPL's lack of destination clauses and flexible LNG dispatch provides greater LNG trading optionality for SPL off-takers.

Natural Gas Supply

US natural gas market is the deepest and most liquid in the world. SPL strategic location close to major gas-producing fields as well as key interstate and intrastate gas pipeline infrastructure reduces gas supply risk. Natural gas commodity price risk mitigated by indexing to HH market price, which is subject to full pass-through to offtakers under SPA offtake contracts.

SPL Project Outcomes

SPL was a groundbreaking project not only in terms of the operational achievements as the first LNG export project to receive DOE approvals and begin shipping natural gas to international markets but also in terms of the financial execution and structuring. SPL successfully brought all 4 LNG trains online ahead of schedule and on budget. Today, Cheniere is the second-largest operator of liquefaction facilities in the world and the fourth-largest LNG supplier in the world. SPL accounts for over 40% of all US LNG export capacity in operation or under construction. In 2019, SPL shipped 325 cargoes of LNG and 1,000 in total since train 1 commenced operations in 2016. The 2013, $5.9 billion bank loan project financing was successfully refinanced in full in the US debt capital markets via 9 different bond issuances over 2–3 years and achieved long dated, 15-to-20-year bond tenors at very favorable fixed interest rates (averaging 5.7% all in).[3] SPL would fund construction costs from the bank loan, and once the project had drawn down $1–1.5 billion of bank debt, they would approach the capital markets to refinance the bank debt, thereby avoiding the bond negative carry cost and ensuring an orderly, periodic, and well-managed refinancing of the entire bank loan. For the commercial banks, the original 7-year mini-perm loan was repaid in full by year 4 or 5, resulting in an average loan life closer to 3.5 years and thus enabling bank capital to be recycled into new project finance deals. The successful application of the mini-perm financing structure to SPL served to open the way for a pipeline of other US LNG projects to be financed in similar fashion.

ENDNOTES

1. PR Newswire, "Cheniere Partners Completes Financing and Commences Construction on Sabine Pass Liquefaction Trains 3 and 4, Purchases Creole Trail Pipeline" (May 29, 2013).
2. The Oxford Institute for Energy Studies, "LNG Plant Cost Reduction 2014–18" (Brian Songhurst, OIES Paper: NG137 October 2018), 4,5.
3. Cheniere Energy, Inc, "Fourth Quarter and Full Year 2019 Presentation" (February 25, 2020).

CHAPTER 7

Environmental and Social Governance (ESG)

Project finance and infrastructure investment invariably entail some level of negative environmental and social impact—development versus sustainability zero-sum trade-off. Global population growth, urbanization, and the existential threat of climate change present new challenges in meeting the estimated $18 trillion gap between global infrastructure needs and current infrastructure investment over the next 20 years.[1] In January 2020, the Global Infrastructure Hub in collaboration with the World Economic Forum and Boston Consulting Group released a draft report on future trends for infrastructure and the large-scale, transformational megatrends over the next 30 years.[2] The report included a survey of 70 countries (35% emerging markets and 65% developed countries) identifying the most pressing issues that countries were most concerned about. Not surprisingly, infrastructure sustainability underscored by aging infrastructure, the increasing frequency of natural disasters, and reliance of infrastructure and the rise of climate change ranked highest in terms of both impact and lack of preparedness. In its 2016 report, "Meeting Asia's Infrastructure Needs," the ADB quantified the cost of climate change impacts in meeting Asia's growing infrastructure needs through 2030 at around $3.4 trillion—primarily the costs to insulate infrastructure against increasing climate change impacts (rising sea levels, increasingly severe weather events, etc.) as well as climate change mitigation (such as increasing investment in renewables).

SUSTAINABLE INFRASTRUCTURE PROJECT FINANCE AND INVESTING

The challenge of delivering the massive infrastructure needs of the world over the next 20 years are compounded by the need to ensure said infrastructure meets minimum sustainability requirements—climate resilient, minimal carbon footprint, and optimized social inclusiveness. The emergence of climate change as a global issue and the rapidly increasing inclusion of ESG policies in corporate mission statements, along with the emergence of institutional capital with ESG investment goals and conditions, has resulted in greater alignment between infrastructure financing, investment, and sustainability metrics. Several studies have attempted to quantify the effect of climate change and the need to improve infrastructure sustainability. The 2016 ADB report on Asian infrastructure calculated that the costs of climate-proofing infrastructure and addressing climate change would require additional investment capital of almost $3.4 trillion between 2016 and 2030. McKinsey studied the cost impact of the $90 trillion of new infrastructure needed between 2015 and 2030 and estimated that the "sustainability premium" to adequately address climate change could add an additional $14 trillion to the overall cost of infrastructure (offset in part by cost savings from reduced fossil fuel costs and urban efficiency). This is comprised of $9 trillion of investment in low-carbon power generation and $5 trillion in energy efficiency.[3]

There have been several recent and very tangible examples of sustainability and ESG requirements directly affecting project finance lending. In 2019, a $1 billion syndicated revolving credit loan facility for SBM Offshore included a "sustainability improvement derivative" credit spread linked to the measurable sustainability performance of SBM Offshore. SBM Offshore is a Dutch-based oilfield service company and one of the largest owners and operators of floating, production, storage, and offloading (FPSO) vessels for the O&G sector. This sustainability credit spread is in addition to the base lending risk spread and can increase and decrease depending on SBM Offshore's ESG performance, which is assessed annually by an independent environmental consultant. The trend of embedding ESG metrics and costs into loans and other forms of capital provided by investors and institutional lenders is expected to increase as lending institutions increasingly embed sustainability objectives into financial return measurements.

EQUATOR PRINCIPLES

The Equator Principles (EPs) are a voluntary, self-monitoring risk management framework adopted by commercial banks for determining, assessing, and managing environmental and social risks in project finance. The EPs are based on the IFC's ESG Performance Standards and provide a minimum standard for due diligence to support responsible risk decision-making. The EPs apply globally to all industry sectors and to four financial products: (1) project finance advisory services, (2) project finance lending, (3) project-related corporate loans, and (4) project-related bridge loans. EP financial institutions (EPFIs) commit to implementing the EPs in their internal environmental and social policies, procedures, and standards for financing projects and undertake not to provide project finance or project-related corporate loans to projects where the client will not, or is unable to, comply with the EPs. As of May 2020, 104 financial institutions in 38 countries have officially adopted the EP, covering the vast majority of project finance lending banks.

The origins of the EPs date back to the late 1990s and early 2000s when commercial banks and other lending institutions were not heavily focused on the environmental and social risks associated with project finance lending. Commercial banks had largely outsourced this risk and relied on co-financing with MDBs, BDBs, and ECAs to set the standards for ESG compliance and monitoring in project finance deals. Several high-profile project finance transactions with problematic environmental and social effects—highlighted by pressure and criticism from NGOs and environmental groups—brought greater awareness to this issue by banks: particularly institutional reputational risks. One of the most notorious project deals that ran afoul of ESG risk was the highly controversial 2001, $1.3 billion, 300-mile OCP Pipeline project in Ecuador. The route of the OCP oil pipeline extended from interior rain forests of Ecuador to the Pacific coast and traversed 11 ecosystems, 6 active volcanoes, and numerous indigenous communities with material impact on biodiversity reserves and endangered species. German bank West LB led the bank syndicate for the $900 million project financing of OCP. Following a backlash from NGOs and several high-profile oil spills, West LB and its stakeholders faced intense criticism for its financial support of OCP. OCP and other environmentally sensitive project financings prompted much soul-searching by lenders and served as a wake-up call to commercial banks as to the materiality of ESG risks and associated reputational risks inherent in certain high-impact project finance deals. In 2002, ABN Amro and the IFC led an initiative to implement an

ESG risk management framework for commercial banks, which ultimately led to the adoption of EPs in June 2003 by an initial group of 10 signatory banks who represented over 30% of the project finance loan market and included the four core founding members—ABN Amro, Citibank, West LB, and Barclays.[4]

The EPs have dramatically transformed the way project lenders assess and analyze ESG risks and forced banks to be highly selective with respect to the project deals they elect to provide loan capital to. It is not unusual for banks to walk away from a project deal if there are excessive ESG risks and/or the project sponsor exhibits a reluctance to comply with EPs. A number of banking institutions for whom I worked had both a credit committee approval process as well as reputational risk committee approval process for ESG risks—in many cases the reputational risk committee was far more exacting and onerous than the credit approval process given the potential ESG-related reputational risks to the bank. The EPs comprise 10 core principles, which EPFIs are required to follow in assessing the ESG risks associated with a project finance deal:

Principle 1: Project Review and Categorization

When EPFIs are initially requested to consider financing a project deal, they are required to review and categorize the project as part of the ESG assessment according to the scale and magnitude of the potential ESG impacts. There are three categories:

1. **Category A**—Projects with potential significant adverse environmental and social risks and/or impacts that are diverse, irreversible, or unprecedented;
2. **Category B**—Projects with potential limited adverse environmental and social risks and/or impacts that are few in number, generally site-specific, largely reversible, and readily addressed through mitigation measures; and
3. **Category C**—Projects with minimal or no adverse environmental and social risks and/or impacts.

Principle 2: Environmental and Social Assessment

Any category A or B project is required to undertake a full environmental impact assessment (EIA) analysis to understand the ESG risks associated with the project including mitigation measures and action items to minimize the ESG risks. EPFIs will generally engage an independent environmental consultant to conduct the EIA.

Principle 3: Applicable Environmental and Social Standards

The EIA will assess compliance with the IFC's "Performance Standards on Environmental and Social Sustainability" as well as compliance with local host country social and environmental laws.

Principle 4: Environmental and Social Management System and Equator Principles Action Plan

For all category A and category B projects, the EPFI will require the sponsor/client to develop or maintain an environmental and social management system. Further, an environmental and social management plan will be prepared by the sponsor/client to address issues raised in the EIA and incorporate actions required to comply with the applicable standards.

Principle 5: Stakeholder Engagement

For all category A and category B projects, the EPFI will require the sponsor/client to demonstrate effective stakeholder engagement with affected communities including public meetings and consultation and feedback. Indigenous communities are subject to informed consent and consultation.

Principle 6: Grievance Mechanism

For all category A and, as appropriate, category B projects, the EPFI will require the sponsor/client to establish a grievance mechanism designed to receive and facilitate resolution of concerns and grievances about the project's environmental and social performance.

Principle 7: Independent Review

An independent social and environmental consultant not associated with the project sponsor is required to conduct an independent review of the EIA process and ensure compliance with EPs.

Principle 8: Covenants

For all projects, the project company will covenant in the financing documentation to comply with all relevant host country environmental and social laws, regulations, and permits in all material respects. For category A and B projects, they must comply with EPs and any action plan and monitoring and reporting requirements needed to determine covenant compliance.

Principle 9: Independent Monitoring and Reporting

To assess project compliance with the EPs and ensure ongoing monitoring and reporting after financial close and over the life of the loan, the EPFI will, for all category A and, as appropriate, category B projects, require the appointment of an independent environmental and social consultant.

Principle 10: Reporting and Transparency

EPFIs are required to provide annual reports of all project finance deals that have reached financial close and are subject to the EP process.

Equator Principles: Assessment and Management of Social and Environmental Risks

The principles:

Project Categorization
EPFI to classify projects based on IFC criteria

Social and Environmental Assessment
Conduct SEA for Category A and B Projects

Applicable Social and Environmental Standards
Projects in non-OECD and low income OECD – comply with IFC performance standards and EHS Guidlines

Action Plan and Management System
Action Plan and Management System to develop and implement integration measures, corrective actions monitoring for the impacts and risks

Communication and Disclosure
Consultation and engagement of project affected communities

Grievance Mechanism
Grievance mechanism in the Management System for affected communities during construction and operation

Independent review
SEA, Action plan and consultation review by independent technical experts

Covenants
Compliance of regulations, Action plan and reporting requirements

Independent Monitoring and Reporting
Periodic monitoring by independent entity

EPFI reporting
EPFI to report publicly EP related projects

MULTILATERAL DEVELOPMENT BANKS AND ESG FRAMEWORKS

MDBs have traditionally been at the coal face when it comes to spearheading financing for infrastructure investment in developing countries given the strong correlation between infrastructure and social and economic growth and ultimately, poverty reduction. While MDBs remain a vital and indispensable component of the financing mix for infrastructure lending, their relative lending prominence has declined or been overtaken by the increasing size of infrastructure investment needs—and the ability of MDBs to scale up financing to meet these growing needs—as well as the fast-evolving infrastructure financing markets and the emergence of nimbler and more flexible players such as infrastructure funds, debt capital markets, ECAs, and regional banks. Political and governance issues, along with internal operational constraints, have also hampered MDBs' ability to quickly innovate and adapt to the fast-changing global infrastructure market. Simultaneously meeting the post-2015 SDGs as well as closing the ever-increasing infrastructure gap has placed renewed emphasis on MDBs finding new solutions and ideas to catalyze ever larger amounts of private sector lending capital. A 2019 joint study by IDB-Invest and the World Bank analyzed whether MDBs effectively and efficiently crowd in private finance by analyzing syndicated lending to 100 countries over 25 years.[5] The study concluded that for every $1 of MDB lending, an additional $7 was catalyzed from private lenders and that loan tenors and average loan amounts were higher when MDBs were involved in the financing. The emergence of new MDBs (the BRICS New Development Bank, or NDB, and the China-led Asia Infrastructure Investment Bank, or AIIB) have increased the urgency for global MDBs to find new ways to collaborate and pool capital and resources to achieve the necessary scalability to meet the needs of the evolving infrastructure market.

One of the main effects on the speed and quantum of MDB infrastructure financing is the ESG safeguards imposed by MDBs aimed at limiting negative social and environmental effects on infrastructure investment. The World Bank implemented rigorous ESG policies in the 1960s, which today form the market basis for ESG policies and requirements—particularly in relation to hot button issues such as environmental impact assessment and resettlement costs associated primarily with hydroelectric projects—of all global and regional MDBs. The IFC overhauled the World Bank safeguards in 2012 to produce a new set of "Performance Standards" in order to streamline the ESG approval process. The IFC Performance Standards form the basis of the EPs, which commercial banks adopted and follow. The ESG requirements of the major MDBs and the associated lengthy, costly, and complex approval processes have become a major deterrent for borrowers. The 2001 World Bank "Cost of Doing Business" study concluded that public procurement rules added 30–35% to a borrower's normal costs while compliance with lengthy social and environmental requirements added a further 40–60% to costs.[6] The challenge for traditional MDBs is how to remain a competitive, value-added financing option for infrastructure investments given the proliferation of new MDBs (AIIB, NDB) or alternative non-traditional funding sources (pension funds, sovereign wealth funds, private equity, hedge funds, etc.) and the increasing dominance of Asian ECAs (KEXIM, CEXIM Bank) and BDBs (Korea Development Bank), which are more commercially flexible and have less onerous internal ESG processes. The other overriding issue for MDBs is the "additionality" condition to lending—MDBs have to offer incremental or additional financing value by not crowding out private sector lending. In a low interest rate financing environment with large pools of capital aggressively chasing risk-adjusted investment returns, it has become more difficult for MDBs to meet the "additionality" condition except for the most challenging private sector projects in the highest risk developing countries.

Since 2012's "Principles to Support Sustainable Private Sector Operations," MDBs have been coordinating and harmonizing lending policies to ensure closer alignment and to more effectively leverage their collective ability to co-finance non-sovereign and private sector projects. The shared principles include, among other things:

- Financing that is not provided by the market;
- Risk mitigation and/or risk sharing;
- Improved project design;
- Better development outcomes; and
- ESG standards.

The 2012 paper was further expanded upon and developed with the September 2018 paper entitled "Multilateral Development Banks' Harmonized Framework For Additionality in Private Sector Operation" issued by all the major global MDBs including the African Development Bank, the ADB, the EIB, the European Bank For Reconstruction and Development, the AIIB, the Islamic Development Bank Group, the NDB, and the World Bank Group (it is noteworthy that the two new MDBs—the AIIB and the NDB—established by China and the BRICS countries are both party to the common guidelines and principles adopted by the MDBs).[7] The paper set forth a common framework for harmonizing additionality requirements—including ESG principles—and how the MDBs can work together more effectively and synergistically to catalyze the optimum amount of private sector capital for development finance while meeting the SDG goals.

IFC IMPACT INVESTING PRINCIPLES

Impact investing is a relatively new concept, which broadly refers to efforts to mobilize investment capital for infrastructure projects that target quantifiable and measurable positive social, environmental, and developmental outcomes alongside financial returns. Impact investing differs from value investing in some crucial ways—value investors seek to invest debt and/or equity in enterprises whose ESG policies are aligned with the investor. For example, an asset manager with a value investing strategy would seek to invest in renewable energy companies while cutting investments in fossil fuel companies or cigarette manufacturers without delivering any measurement of beneficial change in the enterprises' social and environmental contributions. Impact investing goes a step further in that it requires that there is a measurable enterprise impact arising from the fund investment that demonstrates a positive contribution to the enterprises' social and environmental impacts. While the impact investment market is still relatively small (currently around $800 billion), the future market potential is estimated to be as much as $26 trillion (10% of the total $267 trillion of total financial assets globally).[8] Impact investors are heavily focused on infrastructure—62% of funds are invested in infrastructure in developed countries. In developing countries only 9% is invested due to infrastructure not being well established as an asset class; however, it underscores the potential investment opportunities arising from unlocking this investment capital for infrastructure in emerging markets.

In 2019, fund managers raised a record $98 billion in infrastructure funds from investors (pension funds, insurance companies, private equity, etc.). Average size of infrastructure funds surpassed $1 billion and included a $22 billion fund raised by Global Infrastructure Partners—the largest infrastructure fund ever closed. Importantly, fund managers held over $212 billion in unallocated commitments or "dry powder" for investment in infrastructure deals, 50% above 2015 levels. This serves to further underscore both the rapidly increasing investor appetite for infrastructure investments as an asset class and the challenges with channeling this available capital toward project investments. As many of these institutional investors adopt the SDG goals, the relationship between SDG impact goals and financial returns have become inexorably linked when making investment decisions. To meet SDGs by 2030, covering the 5 key impact sectors (education, health, roads, electricity, water, and sanitation) will require additional annual spending of $0.5 trillion in low-income developed countries, and $2.1 trillion (approximately 4% of GDP) in emerging market economies.

Recognizing the growing investor interest in impact investment but without a common standard for what constitutes impact investing, the IFC led an initiative to develop a market framework for investors. The aim was to design a common framework with broad investor buy-in and adoption, which would provide transparency and market discipline for investors to measure and monitor impact outcomes. The IFC also hoped it would result in establishing higher standards and goals for achieving ESG impact outcomes by investors. Arising from these efforts, in April 2019, 60 initial adopter investors and the IFC signed The Operating Principles for Impacting Management (Principles) in Washington, DC.[9] As of February 2020, the number of signatories to the Principles has grown to 84 investors. The Principles were developed in conjunction with asset managers and owners to unlock the ability of impact investment to address SDG challenges around economic inequality, access to clean water and sanitation, and carbon reduction. The Principles were designed to provide investors with a paradigm to create their own impact investment framework to ensure impact considerations are embedded throughout the investment cycle. They provide a benchmark against which investors' impact management systems can be assessed and used to screen impact investing opportunities. The nine Principles cover the end-to-end investment cycle process from setting and defining strategic impact objectives through investment origination and structuring to portfolio management, investment exit, and annual independent verification reporting.

INVESTING FOR IMPACT: OPERATING PRINCIPLES FOR IMPACT MANAGEMENT

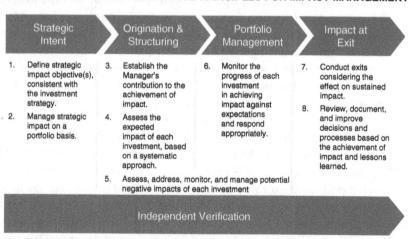

Strategic Intent	Origination & Structuring	Portfolio Management	Impact at Exit
1. Define strategic impact objective(s), consistent with the investment strategy.	3. Establish the Manager's contribution to the achievement of impact.	6. Monitor the progress of each investment in achieving impact against expectations and respond appropriately.	7. Conduct exits considering the effect on sustained impact.
2. Manage strategic impact on a portfolio basis.	4. Assess the expected impact of each investment, based on a systematic approach.		8. Review, document, and improve decisions and processes based on the achievement of impact and lessons learned.
	5. Assess, address, monitor, and manage potential negative impacts of each investment		

Independent Verification

9. Publicly disclose alignment with the Principles and provide regular independent verification of the alignment.

GREEN BONDS

The emergence of climate change as a major global threat has accelerated and focused engagement on sustainable financing and investment in infrastructure. The 2016 Paris Agreement on Climate Change and the 2015 UN SDGs has led to growing interest in linking ESG performance and outcomes to infrastructure financing. One of the key developments over the last 10 years driving these developments has been the expanding growth of green bonds as a new asset class commanding strong and growing investor interest. While the green bond market is small, it is one of the fastest growing segments of the capital markets. Since the first climate bond/green bond was issued in 2007–08 by the World Bank and the EIB, green bonds have become an important investment vehicle for companies and governments to meet SDG goals. In emerging markets, green bond issuance has been on the rise—mostly in China—but lags behind green bond issuance in developed countries. This is due in part to small and underdeveloped local capital markets in emerging markets and lack of investor risk appetite and awareness/knowledge.

According to the Climate Bond Initiative (CBI is an international not-for-profit organization whose mission is to mobilize the capital markets for climate change solutions), 2019 green bond issuance exceeded $250 billion versus $167 billion in 2018 and is forecast to exceed $350–400 billion in 2020.[10] The US is the largest national green bond issuer with $50 billion of green bond issues with the US, EU, and China representing over 75% of total green bond issuances in 2019 (China's total 2019 green bond issuances were $53 billion of which $30 billion aligned with international definition and reporting standards for green bonds). Green bond issuers are primarily financial institutions with the 5 largest 2019 issuers comprising Fannie Mae ($22.8 billion), KfW of Germany ($9.02 billion), Dutch State Treasury Agency ($6.66 billion), Republic of France ($6.57 billion), and Industrial Commercial Bank of China ($5.85 billion).

Global Annual Green Bond Issuance: 2015–2019

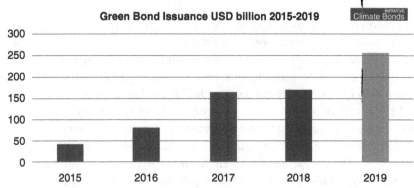

Green Bond Issuance USD billion 2015-2019

Source: Record 2019 GB Issuance $255bn! EU largest market: US, China, France lead Top 20 national rankings: Sovereign GBs & Certified Bonds gain momentum, by Leena Fatin. Initiative Climate Bonds, Jan 16, 2020. © 2020, Climate Bonds.

The issuance process for a green bond is essentially the same as any other corporate bond. The key differentiation is the application of the bond proceeds—in the case of green bonds the bond proceeds must be applied toward ESG goals such as carbon emissions reduction. The explosive growth of green bonds brings with it some major challenges and risks—primarily investor protections, reporting, and monitoring metrics. There is no universally agreed common definition of a green bond. The International Capital Markets Association (ICMA) has developed a set of green bond principles for issuers and investors.[11] The ICMA is a not-for-profit membership association, headquartered in Switzerland, which serves the needs of its wide range of member firms in global capital markets. As of October 2019, the ICMA had more than 580 members in 62 countries. Among its members are private and public sector issuers, banks and securities houses, asset managers and other investors, capital market infrastructure providers, central banks, law firms, and others. The Green Bond Principles as set out by the ICMA stipulates that (1) bond proceeds be applied to projects that have a positive environmental or climate change impact, (2) periodic reporting requirements detailing climate change impacts, and (3) independent third-party verification of the green bond benefits. The ICMA Green Bond Principles are a set of voluntary guidelines aimed at ensuring greater transparency, consistency, and integrity in the issuance of green bonds as the market grows exponentially. The ICMA has also developed Social Bond Principles for those projects that have predominately beneficial social outcomes (affordable housing, health, water and sanitation, food security, etc.).[12] Projects that entail both positive social and environmental outcomes and represent a mix of green bond and social bond outcomes are included as a separate bond category called sustainability bonds and subject to Sustainable Bond Principles.

The broad definition of what constitutes a green bond as well as the issuer's sole discretion as to what bond proceeds usage is considered green can result in bad actor behavior by issuers; for example, despite reputational risk impacts there is no requirement for the bond to remain green for the life of the issuance, and policing compliance is difficult. The CBI has developed a rigorous set of guidelines for green bond certification, which allows issuers to receive enhanced green bond accreditation and validation (https://www.climatebonds.net/certification). The CBI green bond scheme provides certification for issuers and investors that the bond proceeds are applied toward meeting the Paris Agreement to limit global warming to under 2 degrees Celsius. While certified green bonds only constituted $39 billion of the $255 billion green bonds issued in 2019, bond certification has been increasing as issuers and investors seek greater assurance and credibility concerning the climate impact integrity of the bonds as the green bond market grows. The honor system by which green labeling is a voluntary compliance system based on self-policing by issuers has exposed the green bond market to "green-washing" whereby issuers are less than forthright about the environmental impact and outcomes of the green bond proceeds. This has increased the demand for tighter controls and the increase in issuers and investors requiring official green bond certification. Other structural and market changes that have been floated to catalyze and accelerate the green bond market include providing tax incentives for investors as well as introducing margin incentives in bond pricing to better align interests among issuers and investors as well as tighter green covenants in the bond indentures to address post-issuance monitoring and performance on ESG outcomes.

SUSTAINABILITY PROJECT FINANCING AND UN SOCIAL DEVELOPMENT GOALS (SDGS)

The 2030 Agenda for Sustainable Development was adopted in 2015 by the 193 member countries of the UN General Assembly. The vehicle for achieving the goals of the 2030 Agenda for Sustainable Development are the 17 SDGs and 169 targets, which set out an ambitious blueprint for addressing poverty eradication, climate impacts, inequality, energy access, and sustainable infrastructure while spurring economic growth by 2030 (https://sustainabledevelopment.un.org/). The SDGs are broad based and interdependent and include 169 target objectives across the 17 SDGs supported by a further 1–3 indicators for each of the 169 targets (232 total approved indicators) that will be used to measure compliance. The UN estimates that the investment gap that needs to be closed to achieve the SDGs is $2.5 trillion per annum in developing countries, of which approximately $1–2 trillion will need to be plugged by private sector investment. Energy and infrastructure investments represent a significant component of the SDGs with goal 6 (clean water and sanitation), goal 7 (affordable and clean energy), goal 9 (sustainable infrastructure), and goal 13 (climate action) all entailing significant infrastructure investments that will be central to delivering on the SDGs. Some estimates put the SDG infrastructure-related opportunities at over $12 trillion.[13]

One of the key challenges is that the SDGs are extremely ambitious in the breadth and scale of their goals while lacking sufficient specificity and guidance as to how to manage, measure, and monitor the impacts. They are expressed as high-level idealistic goals that are interdependent, and this can lead to confusion: for example, goal 8 aims to achieve economic growth as measured by increases in GDP, which can be viewed as conflicting with goal 13 on climate action. In 2018, the UN (under the auspices of the UNDP) established SDP Impact to develop a common framework for private sector investors to be able to manage and measure adherence to the SDGs as well as authenticate compliance, while also helping identify SDG investment opportunities in developing countries. Most institutional investors have (to some degree) already integrated the SDGs into their investment process. According to the Global Impact Investing Network (GIIN), 72% of global impact investors track and correlate fund and investee performance to the SDGs.[14] In late 2019, SDG Impact (https://sdgimpact.undp.org/)—in collaboration with 40 global institutional investors—launched "SDG Impact Practices for Private Equity Funds" (the "Practices") for comment and consultation.[15] The aim of the Practices is to develop a set of global standards for how investors manage and measure SDG impacts, and in doing so, catalyze and re-route private sector capital flows toward SDG impact investments. The Practices comprise 18 standards covering 3 broad areas:

1. Strategic intent and goal setting;
2. Impact measurement and management; and
3. Transparency and accountability.

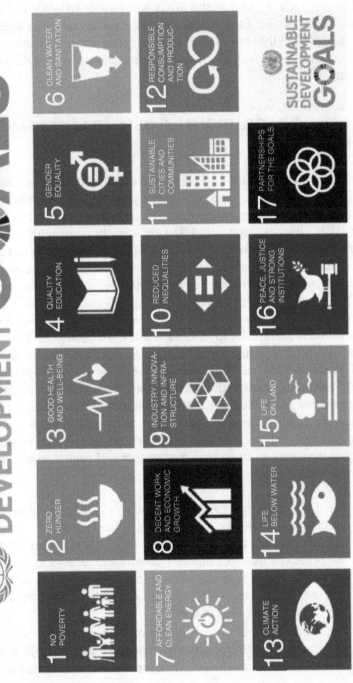

Source: Sustainable Development Goals kick off with start of new year.

There is little doubt that the SDGs will form a growing and expanding component of private fund managers and asset owners' end-to-end investment process and that most infrastructure spending in developing countries will be delivered through the interlocking prism of ESG, SDG, and impact investing principles.

UNLOCKING INSTITUTIONAL CAPITAL TO MEET EMERGING MARKET SDGS

There exists a large capital gap between the 2030 SDGs, which will require investments estimated at $2.5 trillion per year in emerging markets, versus current impact investing capital capacity of $500 billion.[16] In its April 2019 study, GIIN estimated that over 1,340 organizations currently manage $502 billion in impacting investing assets worldwide. Over 800 asset managers account for 50% of impact investment assets while 25% is accounted for by DFIs. As impacting investing has gained momentum over the past decade as an investment strategy while addressing ESG outcomes, the market continues to grow. Other investors include pension funds, insurance companies, banks, foundations, and family offices. While the capital gap is large, there are grounds for optimism that the impact investment market will grow rapidly based on the fact that as of the end of 2018 there is approximately $12 trillion of institutional capital that have adopted ESG criteria and now considers sustainable investments (up 38% from 2016).[17] However, capital flows to emerging markets have to date lagged developed markets. Some of the key challenges—reflective of the more complex operating environments of emerging markets—to unlocking greater flows of capital to emerging markets infrastructure include:[18]

1. The difficulty raising (in the case of asset managers) and deploying (in the case of asset owners) capital. This is due in part to the domicile dislocation between most asset owners and the investment locations and the perceived need for higher risk-adjusted returns as well as differences in investment horizon (most investors seek 5–7 year investment horizons while most investments require 10+ years to realize the full impact and financial outcomes).

2. The education and information gap on emerging markets asset impact and financial performance. Asset owners also struggle with access to transparent, reliable, and comprehensive investment research

and information. There is also a need to develop asset managers' capabilities around investment selection and due diligence analysis as well as a deeper understanding of impact management and governance.

3. The challenge of finding deal-ready project investments meeting risk-adjusted return hurdle requirements. There is a major disconnect between the pool of institutional capital earmarked for infrastructure investment and a readily identifiable pipeline of infrastructure opportunities in emerging markets. The time and cost associated with sourcing infrastructure deals has been a major impediment to increased transactional activity as is the highly disparate range of countries with uncertain legal and regulatory frameworks as well as political risks, which hinders the ability to scale up regional portfolio investments. All of these factors increase transaction costs (legal fees, due diligence) and elongate the execution timeline to achieve financial close (typically anywhere from 6 to 18 months); and

4. The increased costs associated with political volatility such as cross-currency and foreign exchange risks and the resulting need to incur hedging costs. The tyranny of distance between the domicile of the investor and the project country domicile introduces additional complexity and costs managing and monitoring investments.

Recent initiatives to unlock and catalyze ESG-driven investment capital for infrastructure projects in Asia include the launch in 2019 by the AIIB (in collaboration with Aberdeen Standard Investments) of a $500 billion ESG Enhanced Credit Managed Portfolio, which would invest in Asian infrastructure bonds (both green and unlabeled) with integrated ESG factors as part of the investment cycle and portfolio management (https://www.aiib .org/en/news-events/news/2019/AIIB-Partners-With-Aberdeen-Standard-Investments.html). The purpose of the AIIB initiative is to mobilize capital from private investors for infrastructure projects and develop and deepen infrastructure as an asset class in local capital markets while embedding an ESG framework. The AIIB also plans to develop a sustainable capital markets initiative to build ESG investing strategies and expand capacity and Asia investor engagement. These efforts will further advance the engagement of investors in ESG and impact investing–related strategies, while broadening and deepening the pool of capital that can be used to close the capital gap required to meet the 2030 SDGs.

Case Study: Manzanillo Container Port Terminal Project, Mexico

The Manzanillo container port project illustrates how challenging ESG risks, imperfect lender security rights, pre-existing regulatory frameworks, and market risks can be to successfully mitigate through financial structuring and creative project documentation. Manzanillo is also a great example of how two major MDBs jointly collaborated and co-financed while mobilizing commercial bank capital to deliver project finance structural risk mitigation and superior execution. The project also illustrates the application of the A:B loan structure used by MDBs to catalyze private sector lending capital.

Project Overview and Background

Manzanillo is a $544 million quasi-brownfield/greenfield container port terminal project located in the Port of Manzanilla in the State of Colima, Mexico. The project is located on the Pacific coast of Mexico, about 800 km and 300 km, respectively, from the major cargo-destination centers of Mexico City and Guadalajara (Mexico's second-largest metropolitan area). In 2010 Manzanillo signed a 35-year concession agreement to operate the port terminal.

Full development of Manzanillo was carried out in three main phases with the final capacity of the fully developed terminal after completion of phase 3 planned to have about 2.2 million TEUs (twenty-foot equivalent unit) of port capacity. Phase 1A and 1B of the project were completed in 2013 and 2015, respectively, with an annual capacity of 760,000 TEUs and are currently operational. Phase 2, which is to be undertaken during 2016–2021, is the subject of the Manzanillo project financing. The project scope for phase 2 included the installation of additional cranes and the expansion of storage areas to increase capacity up to 1.35 Million TEUs. Phase 3, which will start in 2022 and bring the project to full completion, will include construction of 360 meters of additional ship berthing capacity as well as additional equipment and storage areas to bring the final capacity up to 2.2 million TEUs.

Manzanilla, on the Pacific coast, is Mexico's largest port complex by volume of cargo handled—accounting for more than 41% of Mexico's container traffic as a whole and approximately 63% of total traffic on the

Mexican Pacific coast. The strategic rationale for Manzanillo was based on existing terminals at the Manzanilla port operating at full capacity with draft, storage, and equipment limitations at these terminals, which prevented container shipping lines from bringing in the larger 15,000 TEU Super Post Panamax container vessels expected to increasingly dominate transpacific shipping services to Asia. The new Manzanillo terminal would address these constraints and would have a strong competitive position vis-à-vis other terminals on the Mexico Pacific coast, which would in turn drive volume growth at the port in the future.

The Manzanillo project sponsor is International Container Terminal Services, Inc., of the Philippines (ICTSI). ICTSI is one of the world's leading container terminal operators. It owns and operates 31 terminal facilities in 18 countries, including 15 in Asia, 7 in the Americas, and 7 in each of Europe and Africa. These terminals had an aggregate throughput of 10.2 million TEUs for 2019. China Harbor Engineering Company (CHEC) was the EPC contractor for phase 1A and 1B and completed the civil works (primarily dredging) on schedule and on budget. The major port terminal handling equipment has been delivered and installed by Cargotec of Finland. ICTSI would operate the Manzanillo terminal under a long-term terminal management services support agreement.

ICTSI funded the initial phase 1A and 1B project costs via equity and shareholder loans and now sought to recapitalize and re-lever phase 2 with a project finance loan structure. The $544 million total project costs for the combined project up to and including phase 2 was funded with a $260 million project finance loan jointly arranged by the IDB Invest and the IFC. IDB Invest and the IFC each provided a $65 million A-loan while two commercial banks (Standard Chartered Bank and KfW Ipex Bank) each provided a $52.5 million B-loan. The balance of the financing was provided by a $25 million loan from the China Co-Financing Fund for Latin America under the oversight of the IDB Invest. The B-loans were equally divided between an IDB Invest B-loan and an IFC B-loan under which the commercial banks risk participated through the IDB Invest and the IFC as the official lenders of record under the loan agreements with the project company. ICTSI provided the balance of the capital via $284 million of equity ($224 million cash equity and $60 million from cash flows from existing project operations [phase 1A and 1B]). In addition to the 41.7% ($244 million) cash equity commitment from ICTSI, the sponsor also provided a further financial guarantee of up to $285 million via a

(continued)

(*continued*)

project funds agreement under which ICTSI undertook to cover any debt service shortfall until such time as Manzanillo reached full completion.

One of the key challenges for lenders pertained to the existing legal and regulatory framework governing port concessions in Mexico. Port concessions were assigned to the relevant municipal port authority (in this case The Port Authority of Manzanillo, or "APIMAN"). APIMAN in turn could award or assign the rights—but not the concession agreement—to private sector companies to develop the port services. Thus, Manzanillo lenders could not take or assume any security interest in the port concession as Manzanillo was only receiving an assignment of derivative or subordinated rights under the concession agreement between the Mexican government and APIMAN. The lenders were also taking operational performance and concession termination risk on APIMAN as the legal counterparty under the concession agreement. The track record of Mexican authorities never terminating concession contracts for infrastructure projects along with the fact that phase 1 of Manzanillo was already operating, all required permits and approvals for the expansion were in full force and effect, and construction risk was minimal served to get lenders comfortable with these legal and regulatory risks. Detailed legal due diligence by offshore and local Mexican legal counsel comprehensively addressed these legal risks under Mexican law, and the final security package (which included a pledge over all contracts, port assets and project company shares, bank accounts, etc.) was sufficiently robust and acceptable to lenders.

Social and environmental risks unique to Manzanillo also presented risk mitigation challenges. Manzanillo was designated a category A project under EP guidelines in view of the material social and environmental impact of the container terminal construction expansion. One of the critical environmental impacts of Manzanillo was the removal of 16 hectares of mangrove forests by concession holder, APIMAN, in preparation for the construction of Manzanillo. Mangrove forests are highly endangered ecosystems and protected under Mexican environmental law. The environmental license provided by the Mexican government to APIMAN required the implementation of a mangrove forest restoration plan in a ratio of 1:3, effectively requiring the replacement of 47 hectares of new mangrove habitat. Given this is a legal obligation of APIMAN (as the concession holder) and not Manzanillo, the lenders and the project sponsor had to find a structural solution to ensure the mangrove restoration compliance requirements would be met. The solution was to require the establishment of a mangrove restoration fund, to be funded from project cash flows, which would require Manzanillo to cover any shortfall by APIMAN in the 47-hectare mangrove restoration obligation.

Manzanillo Project Finance Risk Mitigation Analysis

The key project risk mitigation analysis for the Manzanillo project is as follows:

- *Construction Risk*—Mitigated as follows:
  - Phase 1 construction was completed and operating—plus 60% of project costs were already constructed/invested;
  - Project sponsor provided $285 million guarantee to cover any debt service shortfall plus investment commitments up to full phase 3 project completion;
  - Inclusion of a 10% project cost overrun contingency; and
  - Minimal residual construction risk as the perceived high-risk civil works (channel dredging and construction of two berths) was already completed with only jetty and crane equipment expansion required.
- *Revenue Risk*—Mitigated as follows:
  - Market risk was largely mitigated by conservative ramp-up projections based on market study provided by market consultant;
  - Downside sensitivity analysis demonstrated that Manzanillo could withstand a 40% decline in container processing volumes and tariffs while still able to meet 1.0x break-even DSCR;
  - $285 million sponsor guarantee support provides additional backstop debt service shortfall support (ICTSI required to maintain certain minimum corporate financial covenant such as maximum debt-to-EBITDA) until final completion of phase 3;
  - The sculpted loan amortization back-ending loan repayments provided debt service payment relief during critical early ramp-up years; and

(continued)

(continued)

- Strategic location of Manzanillo and sustainable competitive advantages relative to rival container ports.
- *Financial Structure*—Conservative:
  - Low leverage (48%) and robust average DSCR of 2.0x;
  - Inclusion of $285 million of sponsor financial guarantees—of which $169 million would backstop phase 3 investment commitment with $122 million balance available for debt service support if required—provides valuable limited backstop financial support;
  - Sculpted loan amortization to match loan repayment to projected project revenues and cash flows strengthened the financial structure; and
  - 6 months DSRA and 1 month O&M reserve account provided a strong liquidity cushion.
- *Political Risk*—Mitigated as follows:
  - Multi-sourced financing comprising the IFC and IDB Invest materially reduced political risks;
  - Mexico investment grade sovereign credit ratings; and
  - Strong track record of private sector infrastructure investment in Mexico.
- *Environmental Risks*—Mitigated as follows:
  - Detailed and rigorous social and environmental due diligence led by the IFC and the IDB Invest;
  - Manzanillo located within existing port facilities, thus minimizing new and incremental environmental footprint impact; and
  - Project documents require Manzanillo to fund a mangrove restoration fund from project cash flows to fund any shortfall by APIMAN in meeting 47-hectare mangrove restoration obligation.

Manzanillo Project Outcomes

The $260 million project achieved financial close in October 2015 with the finance plan comprising the IFC, IDB Invest direct A-Loans, and two commercial banks risk participating on an equal pro rata basis under IFC and IDB Invest B-loans. The construction expansion of phase 2 is expected to achieve full completion in 2020 ahead of schedule and on budget. Manzanillo has achieved 1.2 million TEU capacity and is expected to increase terminal capacity to 1.6 million TEUs in 2020. In terms of environmental undertakings and commitments, APIMAN has completed over 15 hectares of the mangrove forest restoration requirements and on track to meet the 47-hectare restoration obligation.

ENDNOTES

1. Global Infrastructure Hub, "Global Infrastructure Outlook."
2. Global Infrastructure Hub, World Economic Forum, Boston Consulting Group, "Infrastructure Future Scenarios" (January 2020).
3. McKinsey & Company, "The Next Generation of Infrastructure" (March 2016), 2.
4. *Wall Street Journal*, "Banks Accept Equator Principles" (Michael M. Phillips and Mitchell Pacelle June 3, 2003) (https://www.wsj.com/articles/ SB105467249622739000).
5. IDB Invest, "The Catalytic Role of Multilateral Development Banks in Mobilizing Private Finance," Brief No 10/2019.
6. Intergovernmental Group of Twenty-Four and Global Green Growth Institute, "Infrastructure Finance in the Developing World" (Chris Humphrey, June 2015).
7. "Multilateral Development Banks' Harmonized Framework for Additionality in Private Sector Operation" (September 2018).
8. International Finance Corporation, "Creating Impact. The Promise of Impacting Investment" (April 2019), 9.
9. International Finance Corporation/The World Bank, "Investing for Impact: Operating Principles for Impact Investing" (February 2019).
10. Climate Bonds Initiative, "Record 2019 GB Issuance $255bn! EU largest market: US, China, France lead Top 20 national rankings: Sovereign GBs & Certified Bonds gain momentum" (January 16, 2020) (https://www .climatebonds.net/2020/01/record-2019-gb-issuance-255bn-eu-largest-market-us-china-france-lead-top-20-national).
11. ICMA, "The Green Bond Principles. Voluntary Process Guidelines for Issuing Green Bonds" (June 2018).

12. ICMA, "The Social Bond Principles. Voluntary Process Guidelines for Issuing Social Bonds" (June 2018).

13. SDG Impact, "Catalyzing Private Sector Capital for the SDGs" (Q2 2019 Updates).

14. Global Impact Investing Network, "The State of Impact Measurement and Management Practice" (January 2020).

15. SDG Impact, "The SDG Impact Practice Standards Private Equity Funds" (Consultation Draft: September 2019).

16. Global Impact Investing Network, "Sizing the Impact Investing Market" (Abhilash Mudaliar and Hannah Dithrich, April 2019).

17. US SIF Foundation, "Report on US Sustainable, Responsible and Impact Investing Trends 2018" (2018).

18. Global Impact Investing Network, "Unlocking the Potential of Frontier Finance" (Rachel Bass, September 2019).

CHAPTER 8

Emerging Markets, Project Finance Bonds, and Local Capital Markets

Project finance bonds and capital markets constitute a small but growing part of the financing rubric for infrastructure projects. More importantly, the relatively untapped capacity of institutional debt markets represents the greatest potential to close the widening infrastructure investment gap. As infrastructure gains greater traction and credibility as a desirable asset class offering superior risk-adjusted returns and traditional bank project financing is constrained by ever-increasing regulatory capital costs (Basel III), project bonds will play an increasingly important role in financing infrastructure projects and helping to bridge the infrastructure gap. According to McKinsey ("Bridging Global Infrastructure Gaps," June 2016) there is approximately $120 trillion of assets under management by institutional investors (banks, pension funds, insurance companies, asset managers, sovereign wealth funds, infrastructure operators, private equity funds, etc.) and unlocking even 10–15% of this institutional capital would go a long way toward addressing the infrastructure funding gap. The key challenge matching investors and institutional capital to infrastructure projects is that $73 trillion (60%) of this investment capital derives from investors in the developed economies of US and Europe (with over 83% from high-income countries) while over 60% of infrastructure funding needs are in emerging markets. Infrastructure projects represent a desirable asset class for institutional investors as they offer long-term assets

143

and stable risk-adjusted returns, which serve to match investors' long-term liabilities (particularly for the primary project bond investors, pension funds, and insurance companies). Global project bond issuances totaled $58 billion in 2019, roughly 12% of the total project finance funding market (banks and DFIs accounted for 73% with equity funding the remaining 15%).[1]

Source: Credit Agricole Securities, "Global Project Bonds Market Overview", Energy and Infrastructure Capital Markets Newsletter, December 2019. © 2019, Crédit Agricole CIB.

One of the key issues with accessing the project bond market is its relative unpredictability and volatility as the project bond financing window tends to open and close very quickly, subject to the fickle nature of prevailing and changing investor risk appetite, macroeconomic events, the interest rate environment, and comparable investments competing for the same yield-chasing liquidity. The relatively low level of project bond financing relative to the untapped potential of the institutional debt markets and the failure to unlock this funding and direct it to infrastructure investment is due in part to the following:

- Relative scarcity of bankable infrastructure projects with acceptable risk-adjusted rates of return and the need to improve this project pipeline;
- Material regulatory and investment hurdles. Relaxing certain regulatory hurdles and investment impediments could serve to improve institutional capital flows—Basel III imposes high regulatory capital costs on infrastructure lending despite infrastructure being a low-risk asset class based on low default and strong recovery rates;
- Lack of standardization across projects, sectors, and geographies hinders development of infrastructure as an asset class. Investor appetite is blunted by having to invest considerable time and resources to evaluate projects whose investment frameworks and standards are not uniform and consistent. Having to create unique project structures also increases transaction costs. Promoting greater standardization

and transparency for investors around cross-border investment agreements, regulatory frameworks, documentation, project returns, project risks, and due diligence would help to broaden the pool of institutional capital that can be directed to fund infrastructure investments and help improve matching of investors to projects.

- Challenges pooling projects to achieve economies of scale and weak securities exchanges and market makers to facilitate secondary market trading. Developing indexes and securitization vehicles would embed infrastructure as an established asset class and improve secondary market trading liquidity. MDBs have been trying to act as market makers for project bonds and working to create market indexes and yield curves for local currency project bonds by issuing local currency bonds or providing bond credit enhancement guarantees or bond cross-currency guarantees.

PROJECT BONDS VERSUS PROJECT LOANS

While bank loans constitute the mainstay of the project finance lending market, project bonds represent a potentially attractive alternative source of—or complement to—project financing to bank debt. Project bond investors generally favor infrastructure projects with long-term offtake agreements such as firm, take or pay power purchase agreements or availability-based contracts with investment grade counterparties that ensure stable, predictable cash flows. As a result, the power (power generation and transmission line projects across conventional power and renewable energy) and infrastructure sectors (toll roads, airports, ports, etc., with long-term concession agreements and government revenue support guarantees or social infrastructure under PPP programs) have traditionally tended to dominate project bond issuances (61%). Natural resource project bonds (primarily large-scale LNG bond refinancings in the US as well as gas pipelines and gas/oil storage deals) have represented an increasingly large share of the project bond market in recent years. Geographically, infrastructure projects in North America and Europe have constituted over 70% of project bond issuances, largely reflecting the high-grade risk appetite of investors along with the prevalence of PPP and other take or pay offtake/concession agreement projects with stable and predictable cash flows.

Given their unpredictability due to the tendency for the project bond market window to open and close at short notice, project bonds do not typically represent the sole or primary financing plan for infrastructure projects. Project sponsors will want to ensure they have a backup finance plan incorporating some combination of banks, ECAs, and/or DFIs to cover 100% of the project debt needs should the planned project bond issue not be feasible due to either the lack of investor risk appetite and liquidity or unfavorable bond market pricing conditions. While project bond investors have demonstrated increased project risk appetite, they generally do not like to take construction risk; as such, project bonds tend to be used primarily to refinance bank debt following project construction completion. There is also the issue of the project credit rating requirement and the negative carry with project bonds, which acts as a further brake on the use of project bonds for construction financing. Project bonds can also be financed on a complementary, joint pari passu basis in a hybrid financing structure with a bank loan, where the bank loan is a short-tenor mini-perm facility covering the construction period, and the project bond is a longer tenor, back-ended facility. This can help address the negative carry issue associated with project bonds. Project bonds possess several distinct advantages compared to bank loans:

Fixed Pricing

Unlike bank loans, which are based on floating rate interest rates, project bonds are fixed-interest debt instruments and generally offer very competitive all-in fixed interest rates. This allows project sponsors to lock in predictable equity returns without interest rate risk. Bank loans, on the other hand, typically have step-up pricing and require the project company to execute costly interest rate swaps to hedge the floating interest rate exposure. Project bonds can therefore reduce overall financing cost relative to bank debt.

Less Restrictive Covenants

Project bonds typically have more flexible terms and conditions compared to bank loans. Bond investors tend to require fewer and less restrictive covenants (financial covenants, reps and warranties, events of default, change of control, reporting requirements, etc.) compared to bank lenders. This reflects, in part, the lack of internal resources of most bond investors to monitor project compliance with covenants and the primary reliance that bond investors place on the project bond credit rating and the due diligence analysis by the bond coordinating banks (in case of asset managers and infrastructure debt funds).

Maximize Debt Tenor

Bond investors (particularly insurance companies and pension funds) generally seek long-term investments to optimize matching of their long-term liabilities. Bond tenors of 20–25 years are not uncommon. Bond investors are also comfortable with the bond tenor matching the full term of the offtake contract without the requirement for a contract tail. Thus, for example, a project with a 20-year PPA could secure a project bond with a 20-year door-to-door tenor. Bank lenders, on the other hand, are reluctant to lend beyond 7–10 years, generally require a 2-year contract tail, and—unlike bond investors—will not finance the full offtake contract term.

Efficient Execution

Project bonds can generally be executed in 8–12 weeks from initial due diligence through the bond rating process and final marketing, documentation, and closing. This compares to a typical project finance execution timeframe of 2–3 months for bank deals (assuming project is well advanced on debt structuring with all due diligence and project contracts finalized and deal is ready to launch to market). Bond issuers have two options when it comes to the format of the bond issue: Reg D private placement and Reg S 144A offering. Both bond formats can be used by US and international investors to finance infrastructure projects. The key advantage with either of these bond formats is the reduced securities registration requirements with the SEC, which can be very time consuming and expensive. One important difference between both bond issue formats is the due diligence process: in private placement issues, the investors receive all the project contracts and due diligence reports and conduct their own independent project analysis while 144A issue format places the due diligence responsibility on the banks acting as the global bond coordinators; the 144A bond investors primarily place reliance on the summary offering documents as well as the credit rating reports.

Reg D / Private Placement

Private placement bond issues are exempted from securities registration requirements as this is not a public offering, and investors are restricted to qualified institutional buyers (QIBs). QIBs are sophisticated investors holding investable assets of at least $100 million. Due to the restricted investor base, private placements tend to be used for smaller issuances where the bonds are placed with buy-and-hold investors such as insurance companies and pension funds seeking to match long-term assets with long-term liabilities. Private placements are buy-and-hold instruments, and secondary market trading of project bonds by investors is not allowed.

Reg S / 144A Issues

Rule 144A provides registration exemptions for certain securities sold to QIBs, including very limited public disclosure of project information. The main advantage of the 144A issuance format over private placement issues is the ability of bond investors to sell/trade bonds in the secondary market following a minimum holding period. This opens up 144A issues to a broader investor base and larger security issuances. 144A securities can also be marketed more effectively to international investors as well as US investors to maximize order book building and issuance size as well as achieve tighter bond pricing.

Diversify Funding Sources

Project bonds provide issuers with a complementary or alternative source of financing to traditional financing sources such as commercial bank debt. With long-term bank lending subject to more onerous regulatory capital costs, project bonds can work synergistically with bank loans to recycle and free up bank lending capital by refinancing bank loans after construction completion under mini-perm bank loan structures. The project bond investor base and funding capacity is wide and deep, covering insurance companies and pension funds seeking long-term assets to match their long-term liabilities as well as infrastructure debt funds, private equity funds, and infrastructure asset managers seeking superior risk-adjusted returns. Debt capital market bonds can fund projects from $500 million to multi-billion issues.

Flexible Amortization

Project bonds offer flexibility to issuers in relation to amortization and repayment profiles. While most project bond repayment profiles match project cash flows and are fully amortizing, bond investors can accommodate both delayed principal repayment or back-ended amortization including bullet and balloon repayment structures. This provides issuers with longer bond tenor average life and enhanced equity IRRs.

While project bonds possess several distinct advantages relative to bank debt, there are also a number of drawbacks with project bonds as follows:

Bond Credit Rating Requirements

Subject to the bond issuance format (private placement versus 144/A) bond investors will require one, two, or three project credit ratings from one or more of Fitch, Moody's, or Standard & Poor's. Private placements generally require just one credit rating while 144/A issuances require at least two project ratings from rating agencies. The rating process adds cost, time, and execution risk to the project bond process relative to bank debt.

Prepayment Penalties/Make-Whole Provisions

Bond investors will require prepayment penalties or make-whole payments in the event the issuer prepays the bond. This is due to the fact that bond investors seek to lock in long-term bond yields and matching of long-term assets with long-term liabilities over the life of the project bond. As such, they do not want bond assets to be prepaid. Banks, on the other hand, do not levy any prepayment penalties on project bank loans and in fact encourage or prefer prepayment of bank loans to reduce loan average life, enhance returns on risk-weighted assets (RORWA), and free up and recycle bank capital to be re-deployed to other projects. Arranging, structuring, and loan fees are paid upfront to banks, and early repayment of these loans enhances the all-in loan RORWA for banks when loans are repaid early.

Negative Carry

Negative carry is one of the main drawbacks of project bonds relative to bank debt for greenfield infrastructure projects. Negative carry refers to the requirement to drawdown the entire bond proceeds at the closing of the bond while the use of bond proceeds to fund project capital expenditures are not required immediately but over time during the construction period. This results in the issuer having to pay interest expense on the entire bond amount from day one. Negative carry is one of the main deterrents to using project bonds to fund greenfield projects. Bank loans, on the other hand, allow multiple loan disbursements during the construction period to match loan funding with construction costs. It is possible under limited circumstances to structure the bond issues with a delayed draw mechanism.

This is only possible with private placement bond issues, since you can negotiate directly with the investors, who are buy and hold and generally more sophisticated and flexible. It is not feasible or possible to negotiate and structure delayed draws with 144/A bond issues given the broader investor base and the lack of internal bond administration capabilities to accommodate delayed draws. Another solution to the negative carry issue is to structure a hybrid project bond and bank debt deal where the bank loan is used to fund initial construction costs under a mini-perm loan and project bonds are issued on a staggered basis to refinance the bank loans once a minimum threshold amount of the bank loan has been disbursed. This funding strategy was successfully implemented by several US LNG projects such as Sabine Pass LNG, where a 7-year mini-perm bank loan was used to fund construction costs with the bond market tapped to refinance the outstanding bank debt on a rolling basis once $500 million–$1 billion of the bank loan had been disbursed. Sabine Pass LNG successfully refinanced $5.9 billion of initial project bank loans in the US debt capital markets over a two- to four-year period during construction, resulting in six separate bond issues of $500 million to $2 billion. This funding strategy also allowed the issuer to determine the timing of their choice to go to the bond market to optimize bond tenor and all-in bond pricing.

Covenant Waiver and Amendments

A major issue with project bonds is the procedures for, and ability of, project company issuers to obtain any necessary or required approvals from bond holders for project covenant waivers and amendments. Unlike commercial banks, bond investors do not typically have an existing or long-standing client relationship with the project sponsor; they are investing in the project bond principally to secure matching long-term assets to their long-term liabilities or simply pursuing a yield pick-up strategy over equivalent government or corporate bonds. Project bonds are also traded in the secondary market, which makes it difficult for issuers to know exactly who owns the bonds at any given time and which investors hold the critical voting rights required for the amendment or waiver. Allied to this is the fact that most bond investors simply close and book the bond asset and do not typically have the internal resources or portfolio management group to actively monitor the project following financial close. Dealing with nameless, faceless bond investors makes it difficult for project sponsors to secure the required amendments and waivers in a timely and efficient manner. Commercial banks, on the other hand, provide project finance lending on the basis of long-standing, pre-existing client relationships with one or more of the project sponsors. This makes it much easier for project sponsors to engage with relationship banks—who would be more inclined to work with project sponsors to process and facilitate amendment and waiver requests—versus project bond investors less capable and receptive to providing the necessary approvals. The fact that covenants in project bonds are usually less onerous and restrictive in relation to the operational activities of the project company compared to bank debt covenants should in theory reduce the need for ongoing covenant waivers and amendments from bond investors for routine operational matters. The key takeaway is that project bond investors are more lenient up front when it comes to project-level operational controls and reporting requirements, providing the project performs as projected and as represented to the bond investors and there are minimal issues. However, if the project does undergo any operational, technical, or financial performance issues and requires some level of waiver/amendment approval or even more serious restructuring, bond investors in general tend to be less tolerant and understanding compared to bank lenders.

PROJECT BONDS INVESTOR BASE AND MARKET LIQUIDITY

Project bond investors' liquidity is in large part driven by credit quality and investment grade versus non-investment grade credit ratings of the underlying project company issuer. Although private capital allocations to infrastructure remain small (average infrastructure asset allocations are 2.2–2.4% of assets under management with a 5% target allocation) relative to total assets under management, total infrastructure assets under management have increased fourfold since 2009 to $582 billion due to the robust and stable net returns achieved by infrastructure assets as well as steady cash distributions and their use as a hedge against inflation.[2] This in turn has led to a rapid expansion of the investor base for infrastructure as an asset class. Many bond investors have caps and restrictions on the percentage of bond portfolio exposure to sub-investment grade or high-yield bond assets. There is generally much larger bond investor liquidity and appetite for investment grade or high-grade project bonds. This presents challenges scaling up project bond capacity for infrastructure financing in emerging markets, where sovereign credit ratings are sub-investment grade—it is generally difficult for project bond credit ratings to pierce or exceed the prevailing sovereign credit ratings. The tighter bond investor capacity for non-investment grade project bonds in emerging markets also affects bond pricing and may make it a less attractive financing alternative relative to financing from banks, ECAs, or DFIs. Notwithstanding the challenges with structuring and executing project bonds in high-risk emerging markets, quite a few high-yield project bonds have successfully been issued, mainly via the private placement issuance market. While sovereign credit ratings create a natural ceiling on the credit rating a project bond can achieve, there have been examples where project bonds with structural risk mitigation have exceeded the corresponding sovereign credit rating. The ability to exceed or "pierce" the sovereign credit rating has been achieved with O&G and M&M natural resource projects where the USD-denominated commodity is exported and the proceeds from sales paid into offshore USD bank accounts, thus mitigating currency convertibility and transfer risks and related government capital controls, which tend to be the primary factor constraining project credit ratings at—or below—the prevailing sovereign credit rating. One of the earliest examples of a project bond issue credit rating exceeding a sovereign credit rating was the Ras Laffan LNG project in Qatar, which achieved an issuer credit rating of A3 from Moody's (A- from S&P) notwithstanding that the State of Qatar sovereign rating was Baa3 at the time of the bond issue, in 1996. The key investor base for project bonds includes:

Insurance Companies and Pension Funds

Insurance companies represent the largest investor base for project bonds. There are roughly 40 global insurance companies who participate in the project bond market. Insurance companies such as Allianz, China Life, MetLife, Munich Re, and so forth, are typically buy-and-hold bond investors who invest in project bonds as these assets provide a good matching to their long-term liabilities.

Insurance companies have developed strong project finance structuring and analytical capabilities and as such are able to conduct their own independent project due diligence and risk assessment and participate via the private placement bond execution process. Insurance companies can provide buy-and-hold bond ticket sizes of $50 million–$300 million.

Pension funds also represent a growing and important investor base for infrastructure-related project bonds. The pension fund investor base is driven and dominated by Australian and Canadian pension funds and related fund managers such as Macquarie, IFM, and Ontario Teachers. This is due in part to the maturity of the PPP market and infrastructure as an asset class in both countries. US pension funds such as CalPERS are also active in this space.

Similar to insurance companies, pension funds have long-term liabilities they are seeking to match with long-term assets and as such are buy-and-hold bond investors. Pension funds also participate via the private placement bond process.

Asset Managers/Owners

Asset managers/owners such as Global Infrastructure Partners and Brookfield Asset Management represent the second-largest project bond investor base. Asset managers are primarily yield driven seeking infrastructure investment opportunities that achieve a return spread pick-up relative to corporate or government bonds. The current low interest rate environment due in large part to the 2008 legacy of quantitative easing and loosening of monetary policy by the main global central banks has made infrastructure an attractive asset class for asset managers. According to Preqin, infrastructure assets have delivered a net annualized return of 8.7% over the last decade, which compares very favorably with corporate and government bonds and other fixed–interest rate products.[3]

Asset managers apply a light touch on project finance due diligence and can therefore respond quickly and commit large ticket sizes to deals and ultimately deliver tighter bond pricing spread outcomes for issuers. They are therefore an important investor base for large-scale projects and bond issues via the 144/A debt securities issuance market. Asset managers also create project bond liquidity and secondary market asset pricing as they will typically seek to trade their project bond investment positions.

Infrastructure Debt Funds

Infrastructure debt funds focus on infrastructure assets and represent a fairly new and rapidly growing investor pool. In 2019, closed infrastructure debt funds raised $98 billion, the fifth consecutive record-breaking fundraising year. The largest infrastructure debt fund that closed (Global Infrastructure Partners IV) raised $22 billion from investors and became the largest fund ever. Importantly, infrastructure debt funds have about $250 billion in unallocated investment capacity seeking suitable infrastructure asset investments.

Infrastructure debt funds have created a forum for small- and medium-sized investors to participate in the infrastructure asset class by pooling large swaths of small- and medium-size investor capital into large-scale funds.

LOCAL CURRENCY PROJECT BONDS AND PARTIAL CREDIT GUARANTEES/INSURANCE WRAPS

The development of local capital markets in developing countries offers a potentially valuable and important investor base to finance infrastructure projects. The high local savings rates in Asia and certain Latin American countries has created a strong local pension fund and insurance market seeking yield-enhancing, liability-matching assets. According to the World Bank, the stock of emerging markets' local currency debt securities in 2019 stood at $22.4 trillion.[4] There are two main advantages associated with local currency debt securities versus offshore financing from banks, ECAs, DFIs, and so forth, as follows:

- Local investors possess superior local market political and regulatory knowledge and risk tolerance compared to offshore lenders and can sometimes offer longer bond tenors and tighter all-in pricing; and
- Local currency debt issuances help to mitigate foreign currency risks and provide a natural currency hedge for projects such as power generation, which generate project revenues in local currency.

One of the main challenges with developing local capital markets in emerging economies is the need for sufficient issuances to create a viable yield curve for benchmarking investments as well as sufficiently defined local securities regulations and regulators. The normal phases required to develop a local capital market typically entails a government or sub-sovereign entity issuing local bonds followed by high-rated local banks and then high-rated corporates and finally utilities with long-term assets and cash flows. This helps create a bond yield curve of a diverse issuer base by type, maturity, and pricing, which builds a broad investor base that can risk-assess and allocate investible assets to infrastructure projects. DFIs such as the IFC, the ADB, and IDB Invest have been instrumental in supporting the development of local capital markets in developing countries by conducting capital markets operations in those countries through issuing local currency bonds and also providing cross-currency swaps, guarantees, and credit enhancement to encourage foreign and local bond investors to purchase local currency project bonds. These measures have also helped to establish infrastructure as an asset class with local investors.

Case Study: Project Bond Case Study—Mong Duong 2 Power Project, Vietnam

Project Background

The Mong Duong 2 project (MDP) is an excellent example of a project bond financing in a high-risk emerging market. MDP is a 1,240 MW coal-fired independent power plant project located 220 km east of Hanoi, in northern Vietnam's Quang Ning province. The power plant comprises two generating units of 620 MW gross capacity each. The project's 25-year, take or pay PPA with state-owned Vietnam Electricity (EVN) runs until 2040, with state-owned miner Vinacomin committed to supply coal to MDP at a regulated price for the life of the project under a comparable 25-year fuel supply agreement. The 25-year PPA with EVN, the state-owned power company, as the sole offtaker, is USD-denominated and allows for full fuel cost pass-through, protecting the project from fluctuations in coal prices.

Vinacomin's 25-year coal supply agreement, which will run parallel to the PPA, will supply locally sourced fuel to the facility. Doosan Heavy Industries and Construction of Korea was the EPC contractor, responsible for designing, building, and commissioning the project. MDP obtained a Vietnam government guarantee on all payment obligations under a build-operate-transfer (BOT) scheme, with the plant set to be transferred to the government after 25 years of commercial operation.

The total project cost was $2 billion, of which $1.5 billion was originally financed in 2011 via a multi-sourced project finance structure. The $2 billion project was developed with 100% foreign direct investment. A groundbreaking ceremony for the project was held in September 2011, and the 620 MW first unit was grid-connected and commenced commercial operations in June 2014. The second 620 MW unit was operational by May 2015. The project is expected to generate up to 7.6 billion kilowatt hours of electricity annually, which will be used to power more than two million Vietnamese households. The project also had a material effect on the local Vietnamese economy, creating approximately 6,000 construction and 200 operational jobs.

(continued)

(*continued*)

The project sponsors comprise US power developer AES (51% equity ownership interest); Korea's POSCO Power (30% equity ownership interest); and China's sovereign wealth fund China Investment Corporation (19% equity ownership interest). AES originally held a 90% stake in the project with Vietnamese state-owned mining company and project fuel supplier Vinacomin owning the remaining 10%. In March 2011, Vinacomin divested its equity stake in the project and AES sold a 39% share plus the Vincomin share in the project to its present partners.

MDP is Vietnam's first and biggest coal-fired BOT project and is also the biggest private sector power project undertaken in the country. MDP is the first coal-fired IPP to have been commissioned in Vietnam in nine years. The project is notable as the largest power plant to be financed in Southeast Asia in 2011 and is the first of three IPPs to be procured under the BOT model in Vietnam.

Original 2011 Project Financing[5]

MDP, led by US-based global power company AES, structured the project financing in July 2011 and reached financial close in September 2011. The $1.46 billion financing was provided by 12 international banks plus Korea's export credit agency KEXIM and K-Sure, Korea's insurance guarantee agency. The project financing comprised three loan tranches:

- Tranche 1 comprised a KEXIM direct loan of $340 million;
- Tranche 2 is an 85% K-Sure–covered bank loan facility of $840 million; and
- Tranche 3 is a 100% KEXIM-covered bank loan facility of $280 million.

The $340 million KEXIM direct loan had an 18-year loan tenor while the $840 million K-Sure guarantee provided 85% comprehensive cover (covering the three stools of political risk—war, riots, and civil unrest; expropriation and nationalization; and currency convertibility/transfer risks as well as breach of contract risk under government of Vietnam guarantees and undertakings). The K-Sure $840 million insurance guarantee wrap of the credit also secured an 18-year maturity. An equivalent $280 million 100% comprehensive covered commercial bank tranche was provided by KEXIM. The $280 million KEXIM-insured facility had a 12-year maturity. The combined $1.128 billion KEXIM/K-Sure–provided guarantee cover ensured strong mitigation against emerging market-related sovereign risks for the commercial banks providing the project finance loans under these insurance guarantees. The material involvement of both KEXIM and K-Sure in the project financing was due to the POSCO equity shareholding and the EPC role by Doosan.

International banks signed up to tranches 2 and 3 on a pro rata basis with coverage from KEXIM and K-Sure, which is a key factor in the appeal of the loan and ended up winning support of twelve commercial banks. BNP Paribas was the facility agent; Credit Agricole was the document bank and inter-creditor agent; HSBC was the account bank and collateral agent; ING was the model bank; Natixis, Societe Generale, and SMBC (insurance bank) were book runners. They were joined as mandated lead arrangers by Mizuho Corporation Bank, Stanchart, and Unicredit while CIC and DZ Bank signed up as lead arrangers.

The financing of the MDP project received a number of awards and recognitions including "Asia-Pacific Power Deal of the Year 2011" by Project Finance Magazine; "Power Deal of the Year" by Project Finance International; and "Best Project Financing" by Asia Money Plus.

2019 Project Bond Refinancing[6]

MDP completed a project bond refinancing in 2019 with several groundbreaking firsts. MDP was the first international bond from a frontier market project and represented a landmark project bond transaction for the market. It was the first-ever power plant refinancing transaction or project bond from Vietnam. It was also the first private sector corporate bond from the country since 2013. The MDP bond refinancing also achieved various major awards including the 2019 "Asia Bond Deal of the Year" from GlobalCapital Asia.

MDP sold $678.5 million, 9.8-year senior secured bonds through Mong Duong Finance Holdings (MDF). The debt securities are issued by MDF, a Netherlands-domiciled SPV that acquired all of MDP's outstanding project financing loans.The bond had a delayed amortization profile, with the bond repayment beginning from the end of the fourth year and achieving a weighted average life of 6.9 years.

In parallel with the bond refinancing, MDP also completed a $485 million syndicated loan, which partially refinanced the 2011 project

(continued)

(continued)

financing. The bond deal helped to refinance MDP's existing project debt at an attractive all-in fixed coupon, improving returns for the sponsors and giving investors capital markets exposure to Asian infrastructure.

There are relatively few project bonds in Asia, and there had been very little offshore issuances from Vietnam to provide pricing benchmarks, with no sovereign issuance for the past five years. That meant a complex bond price discovery process was required. Pricing tightened from initial guidance of 5.625% before issuing at an all-in final bond coupon of 5.125%. Even with the 50 bp tightening, final orders were over $2.75 billion. The 144 A/Reg S bond comprised a diverse investor base, with the US taking 32% of the deal.

The project's strong sponsor base undoubtedly helped win over investors. Still, as the first deal of its type from Vietnam, the issuer and book runners needed to convince investors of the strength of the guarantees and contracts associated with the bond.

MDP has a government guarantee on all payment obligations under the 25-year BOT scheme. To keep these protections in place and avoid lengthy renegotiations, proceeds from the bond and the new loan were used to buy MDP's project loan from the existing lenders, rather than refinancing the existing loan. There is a pledge of shares in MDF and security over its assets, but MDP itself does not guarantee the bond, as Vietnam places limits on the total dollar amount of debt that can be issued from the country. Thanks to these structural features, the bonds earned ratings of Ba3/BB (Moody's/Fitch), in line with the sovereign credit ratings for Vietnam.

Citigroup and HSBC led the refinancing as joint global coordinators on the bond and original mandated lead arrangers and book runners on the loan. SMBC and Standard Chartered were joint book runners on the bond.

Fitch Ratings assigned the MDP senior secured notes due 2029 a final rating of BB while Moody's assigned a Ba3 credit rating to the bonds. Principal and interest payments for the US dollar notes rely on payments made by MDP into the offshore SPV under the project financing loans. The PPA provides for capacity and energy payments to cover MDP's fixed and variable costs of subject to a minimum performance level. The project rating for MDF is capped by Vietnam's sovereign rating (BB/Positive) due to the government guarantee of Vietnamese state counterparty obligations.

Moody's final Ba3 project rating rationale was largely based on the following considerations:[7]

- The close links between MDP and the Vietnamese government, given that the government's commitment to MDP under the government guarantees and the BOT contract is a key driver for MDP's credit quality;
- The government's commitment to MDP under the guarantee and the BOT contract supports the predictability of the company's operating cash flow, while mitigating MDP's risk exposure to its single offtaker, EVN, and its sole coal supplier, Vinacomin. Under the guarantee and the BOT contract, the government guarantees the performance of all payment obligations and all financial commitments of EVN and Vinacomin and compensates MDP for any operational difficulties stemming from a failure of coal supply by Vinacomin.
- The rating of the notes remains constrained by Vietnam's sovereign rating, as well as by MDP's risk concentration on a single offtaker and a single coal supplier and MDP's short operational track record of about four and half years.
- Rating on the notes continues to benefit from the major sponsors'—AES Corporation (Ba1 stable) and POSCO Energy, a subsidiary of POSCO (Baa1 stable)—strong commitment, and expertise, which will likely continue to support MDP's operating performance.
- Base-case expectation is that MDP's average debt service coverage ratios will register 1.4x–1.5x during the tenor of the notes. Such a situation will support MDP's credit quality.

ENDNOTES

1. Credit Agricole Securities, "Global Project Bonds Market Overview" (Energy and Infrastructure Capital Markets Newsletter, December 2019).
2. Prequin Ltd., "2020 Global Infrastructure Report" (2020).
3. Prequin Ltd., "2020 Global Infrastructure Report" (2020).

4. International Monetary Fund and The World Bank Group, "Recent Developments on Local Currency Bond Markets in Emerging Economies" (Staff Note for the G20 International Financial Architecture Working Group, Riyadh, Saudi Arabia, January 31, 2020).

5. IJGlobal, "Mong Duong 2 IPP, Vietnam" (Catherine McGuirk, March 16, 2012).

6. IFR Asia Awards 2019, "Frontier Markets Issue: Mong Duong 2's US$1.1 billion Refinancing" (Daniel Stanton, IFR, December 13, 2019).

7. Moody's Investor Service, "Moody's assigns first-time (P)Ba3 to Mong Duong Finance Holdings BV's USD Senior Notes" (July 18, 2019).

CHAPTER 9

China's Belt and Road Initiative

BACKGROUND AND SCOPE OF THE BELT AND ROAD INITIATIVE

China's Belt and Road Initiative (BRI) represents one of the most ambitious and transformational infrastructure programs ever undertaken with the potential to reshape the 21st-century economy. Formerly known as the One Belt One Road project (rebranded BRI in 2016), the BRI was first set out by President Xi Jinping in a 2013 speech in Kazakhstan in which he referred to the idea of reconstituting the ancient Silk Road trading route into a modern trans-Eurasian "land belt" connecting and integrating China with Central Asia spanning all the way from the Pacific Ocean to the Baltic Sea. It would herald the revival of the historic Silk Road trading route connecting China with Central Asia, the Middle East, and Europe and represents the centerpiece of China's global ambitions for President Xi's administration. The ancient Silk Road was an extensive network of land and maritime trade routes formally established under the Chinese Han Dynasty (206 BC–220 AD). The trade route originated in the east of China and connected the Eurasia continent via Central Asia to the Mediterranean and Europe. The BRI's focus is on physical infrastructure investment encompassing ports, railways, roads, power plants, aviation, and telecommunications as a way to close the infrastructure gap and foster closer trade and economic cooperation and integration. A month later, in October 2013, President Xi expanded on his vision for the BRI in another speech in Indonesia when he announced the expansion of the BRI "land belt" to also include the call for a "maritime silk road." The maritime silk road would complement the "land belt" by strengthening China's maritime cooperation with South Asian and Southeast Asian countries and combined would represent the entire scope of the BRI project initiative. The scale of the BRI project is unprecedented in its breadth and reach: it would encompass 71 countries (including China) comprising 4.5 billion people, or 65% of the world's population, and 40% of global GDP. Various industry sources estimate it will cost $4–8 trillion to fully implement the BRI.[1,2]

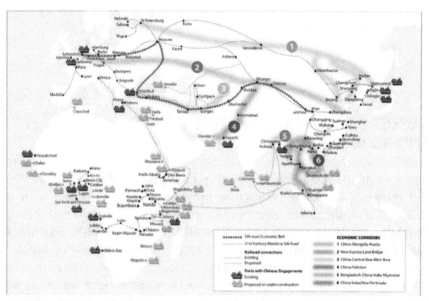

Sources: China's Belt and Road Initiative in the Global Trade, Investment and Finance Landscape. Search OECD Business and Finance Outlook 2018. © 2018, OECD.

The "new" silk road belt component of the BRI encompasses a variety of transportation and logistics infrastructure projects along key geographic areas and includes six land routes with the three most extensive emanating from China as follows:

1. The Northern Corridor: China-Kazakhstan-Russia-Rotterdam;
2. The Central Corridor: China via Central Asia with branches to several locations including Western Asia and the Persian Gulf, the Mediterranean, and Western Europe;

3. The Southern Corridor: China to South Asia and Southeast Asia to major ports in places such as Pakistan to provide easy access to the Indian and Pacific Oceans.

There are four key geopolitical, commercial, strategic, and financial objectives that underpin the rationale behind China's BRI initiative as follows:[3]

1. Closer Political and Economic Integration

China's emergence as a global economic power has led to China regarding Central Asia and South/Southeast Asia as its natural geopolitical sphere of influence. The BRI project is aimed at promoting closer regional economic and political integration and cooperation in Asia via interconnected infrastructure. This would serve to strengthen China's political and economic influence in Asia via "soft power" and serve to act as a bulwark against US and Japanese regional influence.

There are other key strands to this strategy, including development and closer integration of China's far-flung and economically disadvantaged Uygur autonomous western province of Xinjiang. The $1.3 billion Gwadar deep water port development project in Karachi, Pakistan, forms a key part of the BRI China-Pakistan Economic Corridor (CPEC). It would address an important strategic weakness of China—the dependence on the Singapore-controlled narrow but critically important Malacca Strait shipping channel linking the Indian and Pacific Oceans, which accounts for 80% of China's oil imports—while also increasing trade and investment flows to Xinjiang by routing oil supplies overland via Gwadar and Xinjiang.

2. Create New Export Markets

China's economic growth as measured by GDP per annum has averaged 9–10% over the last 30 years, making it the fastest growing economy over this time period. This economic growth has been fueled in large part by an export-driven economy with favorable labor costs. As China's economy has grown and matured, labor costs have increased, undermining China's low-cost manufacturing competitive advantage and driving these industries to lower-cost markets such as India and Vietnam. The other economic change has been the decline in reliance on exports as the indigenous engine of domestic consumption spawned a large service-based economy. Following

30 years of stellar and rising GDP growth, China's GDP growth slowed to 6.1% in 2019—the slowest rate of growth since 1990. The BRI project is aimed at increasing economic growth and income per capita among the low-income countries along the BRI, thus creating new potential markets and consumers for Chinese exports.

3. Address Excess Manufacturing Capacity

As noted, China has experienced significant and unprecedented economic growth over the last 30 years. During this time China invested heavily in fixed assets (property, real estate, and manufacturing) with fixed asset investments representing 50% of China's GDP over the past decade. Most of this economic growth and fixed asset investment has been underwritten by industrial and manufacturing production, which in turn has been underpinned by the production capacity of key commodities such as iron ore, steel, coal, and cement. As China's economic growth has slowed over the last 3–5 years, it has resulted in significant excess production capacity in these key Chinese commodity sectors. The large-scale infrastructure projects that form the lion's share of the BRI project would serve to recycle this underutilized excess production capacity from China to these projects.

4. Renminbi Internationalization

China's emergence as a global economic superpower has not been reflected in its financial status and voting interest at the major global financial institutions such as the World Bank, IMF, and ADB. The Western world's global financial hegemony was borne out of the Bretton Woods system following World War 2, which led to the establishment of the largely US- and Europe-dominated World Bank and the IMF. The president of the World Bank is always a US citizen while the managing director of the IMF is always a European appointment, and more importantly, the US has the largest voting block (15.8%)—and with an 85% approval requirement, effective veto power—at the World Bank. Similarly, the US has a 16.8% voting share of the IMF, and with a similar 85% approval requirement it has effective veto power on any major decisions. Notwithstanding that China is the largest global economy by GDP (measured on purchasing power parity basis) its voting share of the World Bank and the IMF is only 5.03% and 6.08%, respectively. Similar to the World Bank and the IMF, the largest development bank in Asia, the ADB, is dominated by the US (and largest regional ally, Japan).

Since its founding in 1966, all presidents of the ADB have been Japanese. The US (12.75% voting share) and Japan (12.75% voting share) have the largest voting blocks in the ADB and effective veto power. China's current voting interest in the ADB stands at 5.4%. China's frustration at not having its global economic status mirrored in voting power in the major global financial institutions and the US's efforts to stymie China's challenge to the US's hegemony of the global financial system, dominated by the US dollar as the international clearance and trade settlement currency, led to China pursuing a new strategic approach of which the BRI is a key lynchpin.[4]

China has targeted financing the BRI infrastructure projects in Chinese local currency renminbi (RMB) via funding from Chinese commercial banks, government-backed development banks, and investment funds. BRI will serve to accelerate the internationalization of the RMB as a trade and investment currency between China and the 70-odd BRI countries. The BRI initiative and the central role of China in regional trade and investment has resulted in regional central banks shifting focus to respective cross-currency relationship with the RMB and resulted in setting currency trading bands to manage cross-currency FX rates. This has reduced the risk perception of RMB loans and trade settlements relative to the US dollar. Chinese financial institutions have put in place the financial infrastructure to lower the cost and challenges of using the RMB as a loan and trade settlement currency and facilitated the internationalization of the RMB by executing over 35 cross-currency swap agreements with BRI countries. These currency swap agreements will facilitate RMB loans by Chinese banks and financial institutions to BRI projects and will also allow Asian and other regional central banks to approve RMB payments for loans and trade with China. This will in turn ease and expand trade flows and bilateral currency settlements in RMB.[5] China's strategy to challenge the hegemonic status of the US dollar financial system by establishing the RMB as an alternative international settlement reserve and trade currency is underpinned by China's recent launch of several key financial institutions, which will be central to financing the BRI—the Asian Infrastructure Investment Bank (AIIB) discussed below along with the NDB (the BRICS development bank) and the Silk Road Fund.[6]

•Infrastructure Needs of the Belt and Road Initiative—Spotlight on the China-Pakistan Economic Corridor

The China-Pakistan Economic Corridor (CPEC) is one of the largest and most advanced components of the BRI initiative. CPEC is the most advanced in terms of physical implementation of any of the BRI segments and is the centerpiece and a major strategic plank in China's BRI strategy linking land and seaborne trade between China, the Middle East, Africa, and Europe. The interconnected CPEC infrastructure projects will provide China with an alternate route for energy supplies as well as spur trade, economic development, and increased national and regional integration in China's western provinces—in particular the autonomous Xinjiang province. Pakistan stands to gain from large foreign direct investment and the upgrade of critical highway and railway transportation infrastructure as well as improved energy supply and the elimination of electricity shortages, which historically have been major constraints on economic growth. The central importance of CPEC to China is reflected by its inclusion as part of China's 13th five-year development plan.

The CPEC was first announced in 2015 and currently amounts to over $62 billion of various transportation and energy infrastructure projects, including $11 billon for railway and highway transportation projects and $33 billion for energy projects (power generation, pipelines, LNG, etc.).[7] The upgrade and expansion of Pakistan's rail and highway transportation network will link the ports of Gwadar and Karachi with northern Pakistan and ultimately extend to the western Chinese province of Xinjiang. The $1.3 billion Gwadar port development project is the lynchpin to China's strategy to mitigate dependency on the politically sensitive Malacca Strait: a shipping channel that currently accounts for 80% of China's Middle East oil imports. The 3,200 km railway and highway route between the Chinese city of Kashgar in Xinjiang to the Pakistan port of Gwadar will provide trade and energy access to the Arabian Sea and circumvent the need to ship oil imports via the Malacca Strait. CPEC also includes the development of special economic zones across Pakistan to promote greater industrialization of Pakistan's economy.

According to the Chinese embassy in Pakistan, over the past 5 years 11 CPEC projects have been completed and 11 projects are under construction.[8] The total investments of these 22 completed and advanced-stage infrastructure projects totals $18.9 billion with a further 20 projects in the pipeline. The Gwadar port project commenced initial operations in late 2016 while a large number of power generation projects were completed in 2017. The four key investment arenas covered by CPEC include:

Energy: Energy investment projects in power generation and transmission lines is the largest component of the CPEC plan, accounting for about 55% of total CPEC investments. The CPEC includes $33 billion worth of power generation plants and transmission line projects. Most (about two-thirds) of newly installed power generation will be coal-fired, with hydro, solar, and wind energy also forming part of the energy matrix.[9] There are 15 energy projects planned with expected total installed generation capacity of 11,190 MW. Implementation of all power generation projects announced and planned under the CPEC plan would represent about 40% of Pakistan's existing installed generating capacity and would reduce and eliminate Pakistan's current power generation gap and persistent rolling brownouts, which are estimated to reduce GDP by 2–2.5%. Seven power generation projects have been completed and in operation and six are under construction, representing a combined total generation capacity of almost 7,000 MW. Completed power generation projects have already added 3,240 MW to Pakistan's existing installed generation capacity, amounting to more than 11% of the current total installed capacity of 29,000 MW.

Transportation Infrastructure: Railway and highway projects amount to $11 billion of investment. The main transportation artery of Gwadar Port to Kashgar forms the basis for the key rail and highway project upgrades and investments.

Gwadar Port: $1.3 billion deep-water port expansion and upgrade to facilitate trade flows from western China and Africa and the Middle East as well as Middle Eastern oil imports via the Arabian sea for onward transportation to Xinjiang province.

Special Economic Zones (SEZ): Establishment of nine separate SEZs across Pakistan to promote manufacturing industrialization and investment by Chinese investors supported by financial and economic incentives (tax concessions and tax holidays).

An important driver for Chinese companies investing in CPEC projects is the financing support provided by Chinese financial institutions, primarily Chinese policy banks such as China Development Bank (CDB) and CEXIM as well as commercial banks such as ICBC and Bank of China. Another key Chinese financial institution is the China Export and Credit Insurance Guarantee Corporation (Sinosure), which underwrites insurance policies against political risks and sovereign breach of contract risks to facilitate Chinese financial institutions lending to CPEC projects. Chinese state-owned financial institutions are being encouraged to support Chinese construction companies and equipment manufacturers and suppliers (specifically the export of excess domestic power generation equipment production capacity) as part of China's industrial strategy to recycle idle domestic industrial production capacity in critical sectors toward BRI infrastructure projects.

One of the major concerns raised by the BRI is the debt sustainability for the low-income, underdeveloped countries who are assuming the debt repayment risks and sovereign guarantee obligations provided to Chinese financial institutions.[10] The accusation leveled at China is that it is attempting to ensnare low-income countries in a debt trap by saddling them with unsustainable levels of Chinese infrastructure loans and sovereign guarantees, while pressing these countries to purchase Chinese equipment and enter into EPC contracts with major Chinese construction companies. There are also concerns that China could use the loan obligations to exert political leverage with BRI-connected countries via these highly strategic infrastructure assets. Pakistan falls within the category of countries vulnerable to this "debt trap." According to the IMF, Pakistan has an income per capita of $1,463 and a poverty rate index of 29.5% along with a debt-to-GDP ratio projected to hit 80.5% in 2020 (up from 65.7% five years ago).[11] Pakistan's total external debt was $87.2 billion as of December 2019, of which Chinese debt accounts for just over $22 billion, or 25.5% of Pakistan's total debt. Perhaps more relevant to the debt sustainability question is the fact that $14.6 billion of China loans (including all of China's $6.7 billion of commercial loans) are due and repayable between 2019 and 2023; this represents over 38% of Pakistan's total sovereign debt repayment obligations of $38.3 billion over the same 2019–2023 period. A key component of CPEC-related sovereign debt obligations that is not captured are the contingent government of Pakistan guarantees provided to credit-enhance the power purchaser's payment obligations. These sovereign guarantees related to a number of power generation projects are being developed and financed on a project finance basis using SPV project companies. The government of Pakistan is liable for nonpayment by the electricity power purchaser (in the case of Pakistan it is the country's sole electricity buyer, The Central Power Purchasing Authority) under the long-term PPAs as well as any potential termination payments due under the PPAs. The table below provides a summary of the financing sources for the key energy project under CPEC being funded via project finance:[12]

Sample CPEC Project Financings

Project Name	Debt to Equity	Project Lenders	Project Sponsors	Project Loan (USD millions)
Port Qasim Coal Plant	75:25	China Eximbank	PowerChina, Al Mirqab Group	1,550
Suki Kinari Hydropower Plant	75:25	China Eximbank, ICBC	SK Hydro, Gezhouba Group	1,350
Sahiwal Coal Plant	80:20	ICBC	Shandong Ruyi, Huaneng Group	1,456
Engro Thar Black II Coal Plant	70:30	China Development Bank, ICBC, China Construction Bank	Engro Powergen, CMEC, Habib Bank, Liberty Mills Ltd	820
Dawood Wind Project	70:30	ICBC	Hydro China Dawood	78
Karot Hydropower Plant	80:20	IFC, Silk Road Fund, China Eximbank, China Development Bank	Three Gorges South Asia Investment, Associated Technologies of Pakistan	1,600
Karakoram Highway Project	90:10	China Eximbank,	Pakistan Highway Authority	1,170
Matiari-Lahore Transmission Line Project	80:20		State Grid Corporation of China	1,600
UEP Wind Project	75:25	China Development Bank	United Energy Group	252

Source: Based on Belt and Road Initiative website, https://www.beltroad-initiative.com/

Due to debt sustainability concerns and following pushback from the Pakistan government over Chinese lending institutions' loan terms and conditions, China agreed to modify commercial interest rates on a large number of CPEC funding loans to include more concessionary loan terms, interest-free loans, and grants. Specifically, China agreed that $11 billion of CPEC infrastructure loans provided by CEXIM, CDB, and ICBC—which attracted interest rates of 3%—would be amended to offer 1.6% concessionary interest rates.[13] The Chinese government also announced in 2015 that approximately $757 million of loans for Gwadar Port projects would be converted to 0% interest rate concessionary loan terms, including about $230 million of grants for Gwadar Airport, which are not required to be repaid.[14]

CHINA'S FINANCING STRATEGY FOR BRI INFRASTRUCTURE DEVELOPMENT

Estimates put the potential cost of the investment projects associated with BRI at between $4 trillion and $8 trillion. Financial support will be critical to the successful implementation of the BRI. China has already begun to put in place the financial architecture to support the large-scale lending from Chinese financial institutions, which will be required to actualize these infrastructure projects. Chinese policy banks such as CEXIM and CDB along with commercial banks such as Bank of China and ICBC have already funded billions of dollars for BRI-related projects. RWR Advisory, a Washington-based consultancy, estimated that total announced lending by Chinese financial institutions to BRI projects between 2013 and April 2020 amounted to over US460 billion.[15] Although the use of the RMB to fund BRI projects has been to date low, an increasing number of projects are using the RMB to invest and fund BRI projects. China has reinforced its BRI funding firepower with the establishment in 2014 of a number of new bilateral and multilateral financial institutions:

- The Asian Infrastructure Investment Bank: global MDB with initial capital of $100 billion (the AIIB is further discussed in a separate section below);
- The NDB: the BRICS development bank with initial capital of $100 billion; and
- The Silk Road Fund: Chinese state-owned investment fund established to support investment along the BRI. The fund has total

capital of $40 billion and its 4 shareholders are: State Administration of Foreign Exchange (65%), China Investment Corporation (15%), CEXIM (15%), and CDB (5%).

China via the AIIB is also collaborating with international financial institutions such as the World Bank, the IFC, the ADB, and the EIB with whom financing cooperation agreements have been concluded to co-finance BRI projects. Through the end of 2019, the AIIB has approved over $10 billion of loan commitments of which 46% constituted co-financings with other MDBs.[16] This suggests that the AIIB is not acting unilaterally and is in fact functioning as a bona fide MDB both in terms of collaboration and cooperation with other MDBs and the rigorous nature of internal approval processes and ESG policies.[17] The Chinese banking system is the largest in the world with total assets over $40 trillion and the top four banks (Industrial and Commercial Bank of China, Bank of China, Agricultural Bank of China, and China Construction Bank) are among the largest banks in the world with combined assets of $13.7 trillion. The large balance sheet size of Chinese banks provides significant financing capacity to support BRI. The two main Chinese policy banks—CDB with assets of $2.35 trillion and CEXIM with assets of over $600 billion—primarily support economic development and trade and represent another important source of funding for the BRI. The Chinese sovereign wealth fund, China Investment Corporation, also forms an important part of the financing matrix for the BRI.

China also possesses the largest foreign currency reserves in the world ($3.1 trillion as of April 2020). China's foreign currency reserves could potentially be accessed to support the funding of BRI infrastructure projects either on a direct basis or via intermediate funding of Chinese financial institutions to on-lend to BRI projects. The issue with China's foreign currency reserves is that they have declined markedly from around $4 trillion in 2015 to close to $3 trillion due to a combination of a strengthening US dollar and capital flight from China. Most market observers are of the opinion that China needs to maintain a minimum of $2.5–3.0 trillion in foreign currency reserves to demonstrate strong public finances to offshore investors and in order to be able to defend and support the yuan. This effectively limits the ability of China to tap its foreign currency reserves in any meaningful way to finance the BRI.

Financial collaboration between China and the BRI countries has intensified, with Chinese financial institutions having established branches in over 50% of the countries along the BRI and almost 90 BRI countries having become members of the AIIB. China has been promoting the use of

China's RMB currency as the preferred cross-border currency for funding debt and equity investments in the BRI. This is part of a financing strategy to internationalize the RMB as a competing reserve currency to the US dollar and as a clearance and settlement currency for international trade and investment transactions. The BRI provides a platform to accelerate the international adoption of the RMB as a reserve currency given the sale of the BRI capital investments and the fact that Chinese financial institutions will be providing most of the required financing, in addition to construction equipment and services coming from Chinese companies. A number of BRI countries such as Pakistan, Vietnam, Russia, and India are increasingly using the RMB for trade settlements. China has also executed bilateral RMB currency swaps with over 30 BRI countries with the objective of reducing costs of trading, account settlement times, and foreign exchange risks. The level of cross-border RMB trade settlements tripled in 2016 among BRI countries compared to 2014, accounting for 13.4% of bilateral trade.[18] Furthermore, offshore RMB-clearing banks have been established in 8 countries; RMB mobile payment platforms such as Alipay, Tenpay, and Unionpay have been introduced to many BRI countries; and a pilot program has commenced to allow investors in BRI countries to purchase Chinese RMB currency–denominated financial products. While the BRI will increase the global standing of the RMB as a settlement and trade currency, it is unlikely that it will dislodge the US dollar as the de facto international reserve currency. According to the IMF, the RMB accounted for only 1% of global foreign currency reserves—the US dollar represented over 60%. Equally, the RMB is only used for 2% of global payments.

EMERGENCE OF NEW MULTILATERAL DEVELOPMENT BANKS—FOCUS ON THE ASIA INFRASTRUCTURE INVESTMENT BANK

The launch of both the NDB and the AIIB in 2014 represented the first time in over 50 years that a new MDB has been established. It heralded potentially the most seismic transformation of the global financial order since Bretton Woods in 1944 and a major reshaping of the multilateral landscape.[19] The AIIB and the NDB are both notable for the fact that they are MDBs established and largely owned and controlled by emerging market economies—the NDB is the BRIC's development bank with joint and equal shareholding held by Brazil, Russia, India, China, and South Africa, while China is the largest controlling shareholder in the AIIB. Both the NDB and the AIIB were borne out of a shared frustration with the voting structures and lack of proportional representation by developing countries in Western and Japanese-led global financial institutions such as the World Bank, the IMF, and the ADB and represent a major step in the strategic financial rivalry between the West and the East. Both the NDB and the AIIB have a joint mandate to address the increasing need for infrastructure investment, with the AIIB focused on Asian regional member countries, which largely map to the BRI countries, while the NDB is focused on infrastructure needs in the BRIC member countries.

Asia Infrastructure Investment Bank and the BRI

In January 2016 when the AIIB officially commenced operations it became the first new MDB since the ADB was established in 1966. The purpose and mission of the AIIB is to support cross-border infrastructure financing and investment across Asia and to address the estimated $26 trillion infrastructure gap among Asian countries by 2030. The AIIB is also a key financial player in support of China's $4–8 trillion BRI aimed at bringing infrastructure investment to over 70 countries across Central and South/Southeast Asia as well as Eastern Europe and East Africa in an effort to promote greater regional trade and investment. The AIIB was established with an initial capital base of $100 billion committed by China. The AIIB also represented a diplomatic and geopolitical coup by China as it succeeded in enlisting 100 member countries in spite of strenuous efforts by the US to dissuade European allies from joining. Even staunch US allies Korea and Australia joined the AIIB, leaving just the US and Japan as the only outsiders. Today China holds the largest voting share in the AIIB at 26% followed by India (7.5%) and Russia (5.9%). Asia regional members will hold a minimum 75% voting control.

The history and background leading to the creation of the AIIB is important to understand. The traditional MDBs, which emerged from the Bretton Woods convention in 1944, were the World Bank and the IMF, and these financial institutions underwrote the global financial system up to today, largely under the control and influence of the US. China's rise as a global economic power over the last few decades to become the second-largest economy by GDP (number one when measured on purchasing power parity basis) challenged the existing status quo of Western hegemony of global financial markets as China sought increased voting quotas in both organizations to match its economic standing. The US consistently blocked and rebuffed China's efforts. In the IMF for example, the US holds a 16.5% voting quota compared to China's 6.09% voting quota giving the US an effective veto rights as 85% approval is required to pass any changes at the IMF. Similarly, the US holds the largest 15.85% voting quota in the World Bank compared to China's 4.42%; even Japan, which is a much smaller economy, maintains a 6.84% World Bank voting quota. The regional development bank for Asia—the ADB—is similarly controlled and dominated by the US and Japan with 15.7% and 15.6% voting blocks, respectively, while China's voting quota is 5.5%. The culmination of China's frustrations at not obtaining a level of voting control in existing MDBs commensurate to its new global economic status ultimately led, in large part, to the decision to establish the AIIB. However, there were a number of other reasons why the AIIB was established by China as follows:

1. The need to fund Asia's growing infrastructure gap estimated at $26 trillion by 2030 ("Meeting Asia's Infrastructure Needs," ADB, 2017);

2. Over the past 30 years China has achieved unprecedented economic growth with annual average GDP growth of 9.91% largely driven by fixed asset investment (50% of China's GDP) on the back of industrial sector growth and the production of commodities (coal, steel, oil, and cement). GDP for 2018 slowed to 6.4% as the need for fixed asset investment declined, resulting in underutilized industrial production capacity. China's BRI is key to recycling this underutilized industrial capacity and excess commodity production into new infrastructure projects and the AIIB is a critical source of financing for the BRI;

3. The BRI and the AIIB are also strategic to China's efforts to internationalize the official currency, the RMB, as a market-clearing currency for trade and services. This is largely to create a currency bulwark against the hegemony of the US dollar as the official reserve currency for international trade and financing; and

4. The BRI and the AIIB are also strategically important to China's initiative to achieve closer political and economic regional integration and cooperation aimed at boosting trade and exports and creating new exports markets for Chinese goods and services.

ENDNOTES

1. *The Economist*, "Our bulldozers, our rules" (July 2, 2016) https://www.economist.com/china/2016/07/02/our-bulldozers-our-rules.

2. Ejinsight, "Getting Lost in One Belt, One Road" (April 12, 2016) https://www.ejinsight.com/eji/article/id/1281194/20160412-getting-lost-one-belt-one-road.

3. Yakov Silin, Larisa Kapustina, Italo Trevisan, and Andrei Drevalev, "China's economic interests in the 'One Belt One Road' Initiative" (SHS Web of Conferences 39 2017).

4. *The Diplomat*, "The AIIB and the NDB: The End of Multilateralism or a New Beginning?" (Jonathan Dove April 26, 2016).

5. *Global Finance* magazine, "One Belt, One Road, One Currency" (Joshua Bateman June 1, 2018).

6. *Journal of Contemporary China*, "Motivations behind China's One Belt One Road and Establishment of Asia Infrastructure Investment Bank" (Hong Yu, 2017).

7. Columbia SIPA Center ON Global Energy Policy, "The China-Pakistan Economic Corridor Power Projects: Insights Into Environmental and Debt Sustainability" (Erica Downs, October 2019).

8. Chinese Embassy in Pakistan, "Latest Progress on the CPEC" (Press Release December 29, 2018).

9. Columbia SIPA Center ON Global Energy Policy, "The China-Pakistan Economic Corridor Power Projects: Insights Into Environmental and Debt Sustainability" (Erica Downs October 2019).

10. *The News International*, "CPEC and Pakistan's debt burden" (November 17, 2019).

11. International Monetary Fund, "First Review of Pakistan's Extended Fund Facility" (IMF Country Report No 19/380 December 4, 2019).

12. Belt and Road Initiative website, https://www.beltroad-initiative.com/.

13. *Business Recorder*, "Economic corridor: China to extend assistance at 1.6 percent interest rate" (Naveed Butt, September 3, 2015), https://web.archive.org/web/20151117081205/http://www.brecorder.com/market-data/stocks-a-bonds/0/1223449/.

14. *Dawn* newspaper, "CPEC 2018 Summit: Is Pakistan ready to make the right choices?" (Abdul Hafeez Shaikh), https://www.dawn.com/news/1409722/cpec-2018-summit-is-pakistan-ready-to-make-the-right-choices.

15. *Financial Times*, "China faces wave of calls for debt relief on Belt and Road projects" (James Kynge and Sun Yu, April 30, 2020), https://www.ft.com/content/5a3192be-27c6-4fe7-87e7-78d4158bd39b.

16. Asia Infrastructure Investment Bank, "Update November 2019" (Investor Presentation, November 14, 2019).

17. The Brookings Institute, "Is China's Development Finance a Challenge to the International Order" (David Dollar, Senior Fellow and John L Thornton China Center JCER Conference, Tokyo, October 2017).

18. People's Bank of China and City of London Corporation, "Building an Investment and Financing System for the Belt and Road Initiative" (September 2018).

19. *Monthly Review*, "One Belt One Road. China's Strategy for a New Global Financial Order" (Sit Tsui, Erebus Wong, Lau Kin Chi, and Wen Tiejun, 2017).

CHAPTER 10

Project Finance Market Developments and Finance Structures

The fundamental principles and tools used by project finance practitioners to address financial structuring and risk analysis, allocation, and mitigation have remained relatively unchanged over many years. However, there have been several new and innovative project finance market developments in recent years that merit mention as follows:

MINI-PERM FINANCING STRUCTURES

Prior to the 2008 financial crisis, debt capacity (both bank lending and project bonds) and debt tenors exhibited strong liquidity and credit capacity/availability as well as low cost of capital. The 2008 financial crisis had a double effect on both the bank lending market and the bond market. After 2008, bank lending capacity dried up as banks hoarded capital to buttress expected loan losses and reserved selective lending commitments for key clients. The other outcome of this was the decline in bank appetite to provide underwriting commitments for project finance deals due to the disappearance of the secondary loan syndication market and the resulting need for project sponsors to raise financing via club deals. Club deals entails banks committing loan capital on a pari passu take-and-hold basis, which renders

177

deal execution more time consuming and loans more expensive as terms were dictated by the marginal bank. Credit capacity and liquidity in the project bond market was also negatively affected by the 2008 financial crisis due to monoline insurers losing their triple A credit ratings, which were key to credit-enhancing project bonds and achieving long-dated bond tenors. As bonds lost their investment grade credit ratings due to monoline downgrades arising from eroded credit quality, bonds were rendered unattractive for bond investors such as pension funds and insurance companies, which had maximum portfolio thresholds for non-investment-grade-rated bonds. The traditional project finance model of funding long-term assets and long-term contracts with matching long-term debt was also upended as loan tenors and banks' ability and risk appetite to put out loan capital for long loan terms became untenable. This was also exacerbated by the functional disabling and failure of the LIBOR setting funding benchmark to accurately reflect commercial banks' true cost of funding. As a result, commercial banks were concerned they would not be able to access the inter-bank funding market at rates that covered their real cost of funding. The need to plug this fall in bank debt and project bond financing capacity after the 2008 financial crisis precipitated the increasing popularity and use of mini-perm financing structures.

Mini-perm financing structures—which have long been common in the North American project financing market—enable commercial banks that are unable to offer long-term loan tenors to participate in financings through the provision of loans with much shorter tenors. Mini-perm loans generally cover the construction phase of a project plus three to four years after construction completion, resulting in a typical door-to-door loan tenors of six to eight years. This allows commercial banks an early exit from the loan, resulting in a lower capital allocation and the ability to recycle valuable loan capital. There are two types of mini-perm: hard and soft. A hard mini-perm normally requires sponsors to refinance the loan before maturity; failure to meet this condition would trigger an event of default. A soft mini-perm differs in that the sponsors are incentivized to refinance because the project company becomes subject to increasingly onerous financing terms (such as an increase in the margins on the loans, cash-sweeps, and/or prohibitions on dividends and other distributions to the sponsors). Hard mini-perm structures are generally less popular as they could trigger a default event, which could result in an unintended termination event of the underlying offtake contract or concession agreement. Market sentiment is split on the long-term viability of the mini-perm, as both commercial banks and sponsors remain wary of refinancing risk. Many commentators take the view that a "mini-perm" structure is unlikely to be successful unless there is clear evidence that the project will be able to access the capital markets once it becomes operational (which, as we discuss below, will usually require the project to be able to obtain at least a triple B investment–grade credit rating). That said, if a commercial bank judges that a project may be able to access the capital markets at a future stage, it may be incentivized to participate in the initial financing so as to try to position itself to be in pole position to lead the debt capital markets' bond refinancing.

While the use and application of mini-perms has been largely confined to the US and European markets due to the depth and liquidity of their respective capital markets and the ability to secure investment-grade project ratings, mini-perm lending structures have been used for Middle Eastern power and energy projects as liquidity for 15-year bank loan tenors receded following the 2008 banking crisis. The $1.6 billion Al Dur Independent Water and Power Project in Bahrain was financed in 2009 using an 8-year hard mini-perm structure. Al Dur is a greenfield, natural gas–fired power and water desalination project that will deliver 1,234 MW of electricity and 218,000 m^3 of water per day. This was the first time this structure had been used in the power and water sector in the Middle East. The sponsors and the lenders took the refinancing risk under which the sponsors in Al Dur have to refinance by year 5 or the sponsors will be liable for a margin increase of 50 basis points and a 100% cash sweep for the remaining term. The annual loan repayment profile is based on a 20-year amortizing loan, in line with the 20-year offtake agreement. Under the base-case model, an 80% balloon payment is left for repayment at the end of the 8-year term. Of the remaining 20% of the loan, 10% is repaid in accordance with the repayment schedule and the other 10% is repaid by base-case cash sweeps. There is an automatic event of default if the project is not refinanced before the end of the 8-year term. It was unusual in the case of Al Dur to use a hard mini-perm structure as it is more typical to use a soft mini-perm where the project has a long-term offtake agreement or concession that provides lenders with an assured stream of cash flow to fully repay the loan should the sponsor(s) fail to refinance the mini-perm at loan maturity. Mini-perm structures have maintained and broadened their popularity as they open up projects to alternative pools of liquidity, which increases competitive tension and lowers loan pricing for sponsors. This serves to facilitate more aggressive debt structuring and higher IRRs and the ability to structure reduced, levelized power and tariff prices in support of competitive project bids.

BACK-LEVERED FINANCINGS FOR RENEWABLE ENERGY PROJECTS

One of the interesting developments in the US renewable energy market over the last few years has been the transition from conventional project-level debt financing to back-levered, or holdco, project financing. The US renewables market has some very unique aspects related to US federal government tax credits available in the form of production tax credits for wind projects and investment tax credits in the case of solar projects. Tax credits have a shelf life of 10 years from the start of commercial operations within which to commercialize the tax credits. The challenge with monetizing the tax credits is that small project developers typically do not have the streams of income against which to utilize and offset the available tax credits. Tax credits can only be used by project owners, so it is necessary for project developers to source corporate/financial enterprises with significant tax bases against which the tax credits can be monetized to take a project ownership role by providing "tax equity" to fund project costs. The tax equity investor is a passive investor in the project, and their primary role and objective is to capture the full tax credits during the first 10 years of project operation while minimizing project risk exposure. Tax equity investors are allocated most of the project revenues during years 1–10 (99–100% of the tax credits and a pre-agreed sharing of the project cash flows) while the project developer has a more back-ended IRR profile as they forego project returns in the early years and will realize most of their project IRR in years 10–20 after the tax equity investor has achieved a pre-agreed target IRR. A form of partnership agreement is the standard legal vehicle to facilitate defining the investment obligations along with the sharing and allocation of the project tax credits and cash flows between the project developer and the tax equity investor. The specifics of the partnership agreement (in particular the sharing of tax credits and cash flows) varies from project to project subject to the tax equity needs, hurdle IRR requirements, transaction structure, and tax credit type.

Given the size and importance of the tax credits, tax equity is typically the most important component of the capital stack for a US renewable project, accounting for about 40–60% of the total capital stack. Developer equity accounts for about 15% with project debt representing about 35% of the capital stack.[1] In 2019, tax equity investments in US renewable projects was $12–13 billion (65% wind and 35% solar) with the main tax equity investors largely comprising financial institutions (JP Morgan, Wells Fargo and Bank of America, GE Financial Services, and Citigroup), which represented almost 70% of the total tax equity market.[2] The other key tax equity constituents include North American utilities and, increasingly, European utilities. US companies such as Walmart, AT&T, Apple, Nike, Facebook, and Google have also been increasing their tax equity investments in renewable energy.

A partnership flip is the most common form of tax equity financing. About 80% of tax equity deals in the solar market and 100% in the wind power market take this form. In a typical partnership flip, the tax equity investor is allocated 99% of project tax credits and a percentage of project cash flows during years 1–10 designed to achieve a target IRR. After the tax equity investor hits its target return, the partnership "flips," meaning that the tax equity investor's share of project revenues (cash flows and tax credits) drops to 5%. Cash is distributed in a different ratio. The cash-sharing ratio varies from one deal to the next. However, the project developer typically takes a majority of cash both before and after the flip. The tax equity investor's share of cash usually drops to 5% after the flip, although in some deals, it is as low as 2–3%.

Historically, project level debt was the norm whereby lenders had traditional project finance security and covenant packages (mortgage over project assets, contracts, pledge of shares, insurance, bank accounts, etc.). However, the relatively small universe of tax equity investors and their increasing importance in the capital stack for US renewable projects resulted in pushback by tax equity investors against project-level debt. The concern on the part of tax equity investors is the risk of a loan default at the project company level, which could result in a foreclosure event and a recapture of the tax credits. Today, many tax equity investors will not participate in projects if there is project-level debt, and all wind projects and most solar projects are financed without project-level debt. As a result, the project finance market has evolved to providing back-levered debt financing structures (also referred to as holdco or mezzanine financing) under which the project developer/sponsor finances all or a portion of its equity contribution in the project company via subordinated or mezzanine debt. Back-levered debt allows the project developer to access low-cost debt capital to finance its equity investment, thereby reducing the overall cost of capital. This debt structure also facilitates the participation of tax equity investors who do not want project-level debt financing. Project lenders are effectively providing a portion of the project developers' equity contribution on a structurally subordinate basis to the tax equity investor and rely on the up-streaming of dividend distributions from the project as the primary source of debt repayment. Back-levered lenders' security typically includes the following:

- A pledge of the project developer's equity interest in the project company and/or the holdco that directly owns the project company; and
- A pledge of the rights to receive cash flow distributions or payments from the project company per the agreed terms of the partnership agreement with the tax equity investor.

Back-levered lenders are most concerned with cash distributions to the project developer partner since back-levered debt is a loan to the developer partner against the future share of cash that partner expects to be distributed by the partnership. Lenders will need to understand the terms of the cash distributions and how/when the partnership flip occurs, as well as what events could delay it. In negotiations with the tax equity investor, lenders will typically try to seek some minimum guaranteed distribution percentage to ensure the back-levered or holdco debt will continue to be serviced. The other sensitive issue concerns lenders' right to foreclose on the project developer's share pledge and step into the shoes of the project developer under an event of default. The tax equity investor will insist on limiting change of control provisions such that any disposition cannot result in a termination of the tax equity partnership, which would in turn cause the tax credits to be invalidated. Back-levered loan structures are the direct result of increasing liquidity in the debt markets and the shift away from comprehensive security and covenant packages toward "covenant light" deals over the last few years as project finance has become a buyers' market and a slightly more commoditized debt product. While there is limited evidence to date that back-levered/holdco financing structures have migrated to developing countries, it is a strong possibility that we will likely see these more aggressive financing structures in markets on the BBB-/Baa3 cusp of investment grade where there is significant liquidity chasing fewer deals.

INFRASTRUCTURE GUARANTEE PRODUCTS—BOND AND PRIVATE CAPITAL CREDIT ENHANCEMENT

Mobilizing private capital to address the widening infrastructure gap in developing countries will require innovative solutions beyond traditional forms of development finance and lending. According to McKinsey (2016 report) there are approximately $120 trillion of institutional assets under management (pension funds, insurance companies, banks, sovereign wealth funds, asset managers, private equity, etc.), which are potentially available to be tapped to fund infrastructure investment. Despite the obvious synergy in terms of long-term liability and infrastructure asset matching for institutional investors, less than 2% of pension funds' assets under management are invested in infrastructure asset classes.[3] MDBs and BDBs have developed a number of innovative guarantee products that can lower risk and deliver a credit rating uplift to projects in lower- and lower-to-middle-income countries and in turn catalyze and crowd in private sector investor capital. The guarantee products can be more powerful compared to other forms of MDB and BDB development assistance such as co-financing and direct lending. The positive beneficial effect of MDB and BDB lending and co-financing has been via the mitigation of nonfinancial project risks or what has been called the "halo effect" by credit rating agencies. This intangible "halo effect" or "preferred creditor status" has not been adequately quantified nor effectively messaged with both private investors and credit rating agencies to achieve real and tangible credit rating uplifts for projects. Guarantees provide a more tangible and direct medium to quantify and measure the risk mitigation by MDBs and BDBs for investors and credit rating agencies and thus mobilize increased investment for infrastructure projects. However, to date guarantees have represented only a small portion of MDBs' and BDBs' financing portfolios and have mainly targeted middle-income countries. In 2018, guarantees constituted 4–8% of total commitments from MDBs such as the IFC, EBRD, and IBRD but mobilized the most private sector capital relative to other loan products.[4] Guarantees offer the untapped potential to unlock and scale up institutional investment capital to bridge the infrastructure funding gap in emerging markets by addressing two important issues: (1) scaling up the private capital mobilization capacity of MDBs and (2) mitigating infrastructure investment risks, which impact bankability, credit rating uplift outcomes, and therefore materially tamp down private capital investment risk appetite and funding capacity. In 2018, the G20 identified the importance of credit enhancement instruments such as MDB guarantees as a catalytic tool to better allocate risks and increase the flow of institutional investment capital into infrastructure assets.[5] While both MDBs and BDBs offer guarantee products, MDBs dominate this sector given their outsized ability to influence and mitigate adverse government actions and thus address political risks for investors. In an effort to overcome the limited use and application of MDB credit enhancement guarantee products, MDBs have created a standard infrastructure guarantee approach to foster collaboration between MDBs, governments, and the private sector aimed at increasing the effectiveness and use of guarantee products as a tool to unlock institutional investment capital.[6]

Credit enhancement guarantees provided by MDBs fall into two broad categories:

1. Partial risk guarantees (PRG)—PRGs are generally issued by MDBs to protect investors (lenders and sponsors) against specific risk events tied to a government payment or other performance obligation. For example, it could cover a government payment guarantee against the payment risk under a power purchase agreement or the completion and delivery of critical infrastructure such as a transmission line interconnection to allow the power project to be able to evacuate power to the national electricity grid upon completion. PRGs cover all or a part of the payment obligation due to a specific risk event—typically, a government political risk event such as breach of contract, expropriation/nationalization, war/riots/civil unrest, or currency convertibility/transfer event. One example of a PRG product application is the 2013 Lake Turkana Wind farm in Kenya, where the African Development Bank structured a PRG to backstop the risk that the government of Kenya would not complete a 428 km transmission line to enable the project to dispatch power to the national grid and thus achieve commercial operations. The PRG helped to mitigate a key lender risk and crowded in over euro 625 million of investor capital.

2. Partial credit guarantees (PCG)—PCGs provide lenders with cover against a specific loan or debt repayment by amount and/or time period regardless of the risk event that caused the non-payment event. PCGs are generally capped by the amount of cover and time bound and as such are generally used as "first loss" guarantees to credit-enhance local or international project bond issuances. PCGs can also be used to extend the tenor of a project bond by guaranteeing the back end, or tail, of the bond repayment period to lengthen yield curves and provide better bond tenor matching with offtake or concession contract tenors. IDB Invest provided a PCG for a 207 MW Brazilian wind farm project in 2018 under which $33.8 million of principal and interest with respect to a 13-year, local currency project bond was guaranteed by IDB Invest. The IDB Invest PCG credit enhanced the project bond and resulted in Fitch assigning an investment grade credit rating (A+) versus a sub-investment grade rating (BB-), which would have prevailed without the PCG—catalyzing over $350 million of investor capital and achieving an eight-notch credit rating pick-up.[7]

MDB PRGs and PCGs only provide partial risk or partial credit relief and not full risk coverage in order to reduce moral hazard risk and to ensure investors have "skin in the game." MDBs do not view full credit enhancement of their AAA rating as required or necessary to achieve maximum private investment capital mobilization. Moreover, it may not be in the best interests of investors to have full risk transfer or complete credit substitution due to the effect on investor risk-adjusted returns. The MDB credit enhancement guarantees can be targeted to achieve a credit uplift from sub-investment-grade BB/Ba2 range to BBB-/Baa3 investment grade where risk-adjusted returns for investors are optimized—the risk/return trade-off sweet spot. MDB guarantees offer the potential to tailor the credit enhancement product on a case-by-case basis to meet the specific risk profile, financial structure, and investor appetite and capacity to achieve the optimum unlocking of local and international capital markets. A prerequisite for an effective MDB guarantee program that addresses capital markets investors' needs is a well-prepared project where all major risks (project/commercial including social and environmental, financial, and political) have been identified and a sound and well-defined financial structure has been developed. Effective up-front risk identification, allocation, and mitigation is especially important in attracting investors to project bonds. This is due to the large number of diffuse institutional bond investors that renders detailed negotiations on the financial structure moot compared to bank funding where these iterative negotiations can more easily be accommodated. One of the challenges with MDB guarantees is the differing methodologies for risk analysis and creditworthiness of an infrastructure project used by the three main credit rating agencies. The critical components that credit rating agencies use to determine relative project creditworthiness are:

- Probability of default (PD); and
- Loss given default (LGD).

PD and LGD are combined to derive the exposure at default, or EAD, for a lender—this is the expected loss for any given loan. PD, LGD, and EAD are the critical metric ingredients used by credit rating agencies to determine the credit rating assigned to any debt issuance. The issue is the different methodology used by each of the three main credit rating agencies. S&P, for example, uses PD but not LGD in its rating assessments. Fitch adopts a similar approach while Moody's is the only one to use both PD and LGD in its credit rating assessment, and as such most accurately captures the risk mitigation offered by MDB PRGs and PCGs. Moody's rating approach captures and reflects the probability of default as well as the expected loss resulting from an event of default. Improved harmonization of rating agency methodologies would greatly enhance understanding and consistency among institutional investors as to the risk mitigation benefits derived from PRGs and PCGs and help bring about greater standardization to these credit-enhancement guarantee instruments. One of the other issues with MDB guarantees is that credit rating agencies do not give credit for the implicit "halo effect" risk mitigation via MDBs' preferred credit status. This is due in part to the inability to measure these non-financial risk mitigation factors and the lack of sufficient MDB guarantee cases and statistically insignificant sample data size. One way this data shortage shortcoming is being addressed is via the Global Emerging Markets Consortium (GEMs http://www.gems-riskdatabase.org/index.htm). GEMs was established in 2009 by the EIB and the IFC to pool the historical PDs and LGDs from the loan and guarantee portfolios of MDBs and BDBs as a way to measure the real benefit of MDBs' guarantees. GEMs currently comprises 22 MDBs and BDBs and project deals from 1988 numbering over 9,000 and comprising 1,900 defaults and 2,600 recoveries.

MDB guarantees fall into two broad categories: those that provide a bank-type financial guarantee and those that more resemble an insurance-type guarantee. MDBs provide both PRGs and PCGs under the former financial guarantee type product but can also provide 100% or full credit risk transfer guarantees (ADB and IFC offer PCG with full credit guarantees as a credit enhancement for bonds). MIGA is the primary insurance guarantee provider with insurance guarantees falling into two categories: political risk insurance and credit enhancement for non-honoring of financial obligations of a government entity (sovereign or sub-sovereign) or state-owned enterprise. This insurance product is similar to a PCG and can be used by lenders to reduce the cost of risk capital, enhance risk-adjusted returns, and expand the pool of potential investors. Guarantees have tremendous potential to support the development of local capital markets and municipal bonds in lower- and lower-to-middle-income countries with sizable pools of untapped local savings. Local currency bonds can offer more attractive long-term funding while mitigating foreign exchange risks and delivering superior risk allocation. While MDB guarantees do not offer a panacea to closing the widening infrastructure gap in developing countries, they do represent low hanging fruit toward unlocking and mobilizing critical pools of institutional investment capital on a scalable level. The emergence of a new cohort of MDBs and DFIs in recent years such as the AIIB, NDB, Canada's FinDev, and the US's DFI offer the scope for broader coordination and leveraging of financial resources across a larger group of global DFIs toward mobilizing the investment capital required to solve the infrastructure funding dilemma.

ENDNOTES

1. NREL, "Terms, Trend and Insights on PV Projects in the United States, 2018" (David Feldman, Paul Schwabe, November 2018).

2. Bloomberg Tax, "Tax Equity Remains an Under-Utilized Tool for Corporate Tax Strategy" (January 29, 2019).

3. OECD, "Annual Survey of Large Pension Funds and Public Pension Reserve Funds. Report on Pension Funds' Long-Term Investment" (2019).

4. Center for Strategic and International Studies, CDC Investment Works, "Innovations in Guarantees for Development" (October 2019), 11.

5. G20, "Roadmap to Infrastructure as an Asset Class" (G20, Argentina, 2018).

6. Inter-American Development Bank, "Introductory Guide to Infrastructure Guarantee Products from Multilateral Development Banks" (Pablo Pereira dos Santos, Technical Note No IDB-TN-01611, (December 2018).

7. Inter-American Development Bank, "Introductory Guide to Infrastructure Guarantee Products from Multilateral Development Banks" (Pablo Pereira dos Santos, Technical Note No IDB-TN-01611, (December 2018).

Bibliography

Albouy, Yves and Bousba, Reda, "The Impact of IPPs in Developing Countries—Out of the Crisis and into the Future" (The World Bank Group Note No. 162, December 1998).

Asian Development Bank, "*Meeting Asia's Infrastructure Needs,*" (ADB 2017) Manila. © ADB. [URL or DOI] [license, 8].

Asian Development Bank, "Meeting Asia's Infrastructure Needs" (ADB 2010).

Asia Infrastructure Investment Bank, "*Update November 2019*" (Investor Presentation November 14th 2019).

Babbar Suman and Schuster John, "Power Project Finance, The Experience in Developing Countries" (The World Bank Group RMC Discussion Paper Series, Number 119, January 1998).

Bateman, Joshua Global Finance Magazine, "One Belt, One Road, One Currency" (June 1, 2018).

Belt and Road Initiative website, https://www.beltroad-initiative.com/.

Bhasin Anu, Desai, Mihir and Srinivasan, Sarayu, "Enron Development Corporation: The Dabhol Power Project in Maharastra, India" (Harvard Business School, July 6th 1998).

Bloomberg Tax, "Tax Equity Remains an Under-Utilized Tool for Corporate Tax Strategy" (January 29th 2019).

Butt, Naveed, Business Recorder, "Economic corridor: China to extend assistance at 1.6 percent interest rate" (September 3 2015), https://web.archive.org/web/20151117081205/http://www.brecorder.com/market-data/stocks-a-bonds/0/1223449/.

Center for Strategic and International Studies, CDC Investment Works, "Innovations in Guarantees for Development" (October 2019), 11.

Cheniere Energy, Inc, "Fourth Quarter and Full Year 2019 Presentation" (February 25th, 2020).

Chinese embassy in Pakistan, "Latest Progress on the CPEC" (Press Release December 29, 2018).

Climate Bonds Initiative, "Record 2019 GB Issuance $255bn! EU largest market: US, China, France lead Top 20 national rankings: Sovereign GBs & Certified Bonds gain momentum" (January 16, 2020) https://www.climatebonds.net/2020/01/record-2019-gb-issuance-255bn-eu-largest-market-us-china-france-lead-top-20-national.

Credit Agricole Securities, "Global Project Bonds Market Overview" (Energy and Infrastructure Capital Markets Newsletter, December 2019).

Dollar, David and Thornton, John L. The Brookings Institute, "Is China's Development Finance a Challenge to the International Order" (JCER Conference, Tokyo October 2017).

Downs, Erica Columbia SIPA Center ON Global Energy Policy, "The China-Pakistan Economic Corridor Power Projects: Insights Into Environmental and Debt Sustainability" (October 2019).

Dove, Jonathan The Diplomat, "The AIIB and the NDB: The End of Multilateralism or a New Beginning?" (April 26, 2016).

The Economist, "Our bulldozers, our rules" (July 2, 2016), https://www.economist.com/china/2016/07/02/our-bulldozers-our-rules.

Ejinsight, "Getting Lost in One Belt, One Road" (April 12 2016) https://www.ejinsight.com/eji/article/id/1281194/20160412-getting-lost-one-belt-one-road.

Esty, Benjamin, "The Economic Motivations for Using Project Finance" (Harvard Business School, 2002).

Esty, Benjamin "Financing The Mozal Project" (Harvard Business School, April 15, 2003).

Feldman, David and Schwabe, Paul NREL, "Terms, Trend and Insights on PV Projects in the United States, 2018" (November 2018).

Fraser, Julie M., "Lessons from the Independent Private Power Experience in Pakistan," (Energy and Mining Sector Board Discussion Paper No. 14, May 2005).

G20, "Roadmap to Infrastructure as an Asset Class" (G20, Argentina, 2018).

Gallagher, "Structured Credit and Political Risk Insurance, Report and Update" (Jan. 2020), 16.

Global Impact Investing Network, "The State of Impact Measurement and Management Practice" (January 2020).

Global Impact Investing Network, "Unlocking the Potential of Frontier Finance" (Rachel Bass, September 2019).

Global Infrastructure Hub, "Global Infrastructure Outlook" (Global Infrastructure Hub and Oxford Economics 2017).

Global Infrastructure Hub, World Economic Forum, Boston Consulting Group, "Infrastructure Future Scenarios" (January 2020).

Gray, R David and John, Schuster, "The East Asian Financial Crisis—Fallout for Private Power Projects" (The World Bank Group Note No. 146, August 1998).

Hafeez Shaikh, Abdul Dawn Newspaper, "*CPEC 2018* Summit: Is Pakistan ready to make the right choices?" (https://www.dawn.com/news/1409722/cpec-2018-summit-is-pakistan-ready-to-make-the-right-choices.

Humphrey, Chris, "Infrastructure Finance in the Developing World" (Intergovernmental Group of Twenty-Four and Global Green Growth Institute June 2015).

ICMA, "The Green Bond Principles. Voluntary Process Guidelines for Issuing Green Bonds" (June 2018a).

ICMA, "The Social Bond Principles. Voluntary Process Guidelines for Issuing Social Bonds" (June 2018b).

IDB Invest, "The Catalytic Role of Multilateral Development Banks in Mobilizing Private Finance," Brief No 10/2019.

International Finance Corporation, "Creating Impact. The Promise of Impacting Investment" (April 2019), 9.

International Finance Corporation/The World Bank, "Investing for Impact: Operating Principles for Impact Investing" (February 2019).

International Monetary Fund/The World Bank Group, "Recent Developments on Local Currency Bond Markets in Emerging Economies" (Staff Note for the G20 International Financial Architecture Working Group, Riyadh, Saudi Arabia January 31, 2020).

International Monetary Fund, "First Review of Pakistan's Extended Fund Facility" (IMF Country Report No 19/380, December 4, 2019).

Kynge James and Yu Sun The Financial Times, "China faces wave of calls for debt relief on Belt and Road projects" (April 30, 2020) https://www.ft.com/content/5a3192be-27c6-4fe7-87e7-78d4158bd39b.

McGuirk, Catherine, IJGlobal, "Mong Duong 2 IPP, Vietnam" (March 16, 2012).

McKinsey, Global Institute, "Bridging Global Infrastructure Gaps" (McKinsey & Company, 2016).

McKinsey, Global Institute, "Bridging Global Infrastructure Gaps. Has The World Made Progress" (McKinsey & Company, 2017).

McKinsey & Company, "The Next Generation of Infrastructure" (March 2016), 2.

Moody's Investor Service, "Moody's assigns first-time (P)Ba3 to Mong Duong Finance Holdings BV's USD Senior Notes" (18 July, 2019).

Mudaliar, Abhilash and Dithrich, Hannah Global Impact Investing Network, "Sizing The Impact Investing Market" (April 2019).

"Multilateral Development Banks' Harmonized Framework for Additionality in Private Sector Operation" (September 2018).

Nam Theun 2 Press Release, "Nam Theun 2 Resettlers Have Exceeded the Household Income Target" (23 July, 2014).

The News, "CPEC and Pakistan's debt burden" (November 17, 2019).

OECD, "Annual Survey of Large Pension Funds and Public Pension Reserve Funds. Report on Pension Funds' Long-Term Investment" (2019).

People's Bank of China and City of London Corporation, "Building an Investment and Financing System for the Belt and Road Initiative" (September 2018).

Pereira dos Santos, Pablo. Inter-American Development Bank, "Introductory Guide to Infrastructure Guarantee Products from Multilateral Development Banks" (Technical Note No IDB-TN-01611, December 2018.

Prequin Ltd., "2020 Global Infrastructure Report", (2020).

PR Newswire, "Cheniere Partners Completes Financing and Commences Construction on Sabine Pass Liquefaction Trains 3 and 4, Purchases Creole Trail Pipeline" (May 29th, 2013).

Refinitiv, "Global Project Finance Review" (Full Year 2019a), 2.

Refinitiv, "Global Project Finance Review" (Full Year 2019b).

Sari, Agus P "Power Sector Restructuring and Public Benefits" (Exec Director Pelangi, Jakarta) Indonesia, 1993-1994).

SDG Impact, "Catalyzing Private Sector Capital for the SDGs" (Q2 2019a Updates).

SDG Impact, "The SDG Impact Practice Standards Private Equity Funds" (Consultation Draft: September 2019b.

Silin Yakou, Kapustina Larisa, Trevisan Italo and Drevalev Andrei, "China's economic interests in the 'One Belt One Road' Initiative" (SHS Web of Conferences, 39, 2017).

Songhurst, Brian, The Oxford Institute For Energy Studies, "LNG Plant Cost Reduction 2014-18" (OIES Paper: NG137 October 2018), 4,5.

S&P Global Market Intelligence, "Annual Global Project Finance Default and Recovery Study, 1980-2014" (S&P Global Market Intelligence, 2016).

Stanton, Daniel IFR Asia Awards 2019, "Frontier Markets Issue: Mong Duong 2's US$ 1.1 Billion Refinancing" (IFR, December 13, 2019).

US SIF Foundation, "Report on US Sustainable, Responsible and Impact Investing Trends 2018" (2018).

Wall Street Journal, *Banks Accept Equator Principles* (June 3, 2003), (https://www.wsj.com/articles/SB105467249622739000).

Wong, Erebus, Lau Kin-chi, Sit Tsui, and Wen Tiejun, Monthly Review Foundation, "One Belt One Road. China's Strategy for a New Global Financial Order," (2017).

Yu, Hong Journal of Contemporary China, "Motivations behind China's One Belt One Road and Establishment of Asia Infrastructure Investment Bank" (November 1, 2016).

Index